OIL SPARKS IN THE AMAZON

Dear Doni
I thought you
wd like this.
Regards, Gerry
27.2.20

EST. 75 1938
YEARS
THE UNIVERSITY OF GEORGIA PRESS 2013

STUDIES IN SECURITY AND INTERNATIONAL AFFAIRS

OIL SPARKS IN THE AMAZON

Local Conflicts,

Indigenous Populations,

and Natural Resources

Patricia I. Vásquez

The University of Georgia Press

Athens and London

© 2014 by the University of Georgia Press

Athens, Georgia 30602

www.ugapress.org

All rights reserved

Set in 10/14 Minion Pro by Graphic Composition, Inc., Bogart, Georgia

Manufactured by Sheridan Books, Inc.

The paper in this book meets the guidelines for

permanence and durability of the Committee on

Production Guidelines for Book Longevity of the

Council on Library Resources.

Most University of Georgia Press titles are available from popular e-book vendors.

Printed in the United States of America

18 17 16 15 14   P   5 4 3 2 1

Library of Congress Cataloging-in-Publication Data

Vasquez, Patricia I.

Oil sparks in the Amazon : local conflicts, indigenous

populations, and natural resources / Patricia I. Vasquez.

pages cm. — (Studies in security and international affairs)

Includes bibliographical references and index.

ISBN 978-0-8203-4561-1 (hardback) — ISBN 0-8203-4561-X (hardcover) —

ISBN 978-0-8203-4562-8 (paperback)

1. Petroleum industry and trade—Social aspects—South America.

2. Petroleum industry and trade—Environmental aspects—South America.

3. Indians of South America—Social conditions. 4. Social conflict—South

America. I. Title.

HD9574.S62V37 2014

333.8'23098—dc23

2013014541

British Library Cataloging-in-Publication Data available

A la memoria de Tina y Juan,
quienes me dieron todo,
y mucho más,
para que pudiera escribir este libro

In memory of Tina and Juan,
who gave me everything,
and much more,
to be able to write this book

The idea of an equilibrium between man and the earth, the awareness of the rape of the environment by industrial culture and today's technology, the reevaluation of the wisdom of primitive peoples, forced either to respect their habitat or face extinction, was something that, during those years, although not yet an intellectual fashion, had already begun to take root everywhere, even in Peru.

VARGAS LLOSA

The difference between what we do and what we are capable of doing would suffice to solve most of the world's problems.

MAHATMA GANDHI

CONTENTS

ILLUSTRATIONS

MAPS

TABLES

BOXES

GRAPHS

IMAGES

I started to become familiar with oil-related conflicts while in graduate school, back in the mid-1990s, when studies about the causes and effects of the mismanagement of natural resources—commonly known as the Resource Curse—were starting to appear. But conflicts linked to the Resource Curse were different from the local disputes now rapidly multiplying in Latin America. Early on, during my preadolescent years, oil conflicts were associated with epic economic meltdowns. Back then, newspapers in my hometown of Buenos Aires were full of stories about Venezuela's oil boom of 1973–74, when that country became awash with "petrodollars." The press referred to the country as "Venezuela Saudita." I don't think I could fully understand what that term meant then; I simply felt that Venezuela was in a much better economic situation than we were. At the time, Argentina was undergoing yet one more of the dozens of economic, social, and political crises emblematic of my country, and we watched Venezuelans growing richer every day with a touch of envy.

It was not until two decades later, as a graduate student at the Johns Hopkins' University School of Advanced International Studies in Washington, D.C., that I came across Terry Lynn Karl's book *The Paradox of Plenty: Oil Booms and Petro-States* (1997). That book opened my eyes to the paradoxical connection between oil wealth and economic busts, of which Venezuela later, sadly, became one of the best examples. That was my first acquaintance with oil-related conflicts. A few years later an expanded view, championed by Paul Collier, among others, added a new twist to conflicts related to the Resource Curse. Civil wars in countries with abundant natural resources, such as oil or gas, were now being linked to the predatory behavior of rebel organizations. The development of armed conflict in resource-rich African countries, the theory states, could be linked in large part to armed groups trying to take advantage of abundant natural resources to fund their existence.

As the head of the Latin America desk at Energy Intelligence, a firm specializing in information and research on energy, my task was to analyze every aspect of the oil and gas industries in the region. But the problems I saw in oil- or gas-producing countries were far from the civil wars associated with the Re-source Curse, with perhaps the exception of Colombia, where it was becoming clear that oil was one of the means of funding used by illegal groups fighting in that country's decades-old armed conflict. Elsewhere in the region, however, talk about civil war was very far from the reality of the moment. It was a time when one Latin American country after another was shedding the violent mili-tary dictatorships of the 1970s and 1980s and adopting well-established demo-cratic governments. No one was talking about civil war in Latin America.

I used to spend hours in my work with experts, both in the United States and in the field, pondering the latest oil and natural gas developments in the region: whether President Evo Morales's takeover of natural gas fields in Bolivia was a de facto nationalization; if Mexico's oil industry could survive that country's constitutional restrictions on private oil investments; if the "Petrobras miracle" would last in Brazil, and whether it could be replicated in other countries; and how and when Venezuela would escape the "paradox of plenty," to name a few.

But during field visits to oil-producing areas, I was also exposed to different realities. I heard about conflicts due to water contamination in oil-producing areas, disputes over land inhabited by Indigenous populations, and the frustra-tion of locals promised oil jobs that never materialized. People would ask me to expose their reality in the United States on my return. Particularly notewor-thy was the multimillion-dollar Chevron case in Ecuador, and I did write about that case many times. I heard of similar conflicts related to the expansion of oil and gas licenses in Peru, Bolivia, Colombia, and Ecuador, but these were not yet as notorious as the Chevron case, so editors probably thought them unwor-thy of attention.

I witnessed the oil and gas maps of Peru rapidly expanding, particularly in the Amazon region. I was hearing louder Indigenous voices both in Peru and in Ecuador, opposing the expansion of oil and gas projects in what they consid-ered to be their territories. An increasingly active Indigenous movement, whose rights were gradually being recognized both domestically and internationally, was rapidly making public its grievances toward the oil industry. The specific types of oil-related conflicts I started to witness in Latin America were not being reflected in any specialized literature. Rather, the then-evolving theories about the links between civil wars and oil abundance were not relevant in these cases. These were local oil conflicts that involved mainly Indigenous groups who had a different cultural and social identity from the rest of the population. Such factors made these conflicts particularly intricate.

I soon realized that local conflicts were here to stay. I also felt that Latin America's natural resource–based economic growth of the 2000 decade was being put to the test by these rapidly multiplying hydrocarbons conflicts. So I decided to study them in detail, seeking to understand their dynamics. Thanks to a generous fellowship from the U.S. Institute of Peace, I could put aside my daily work and immerse myself in the study of oil- and gas-related local conflicts. I based my research in three countries: Peru, Ecuador, and Colombia. I had originally planned to include Bolivia, but the scope of the work was intimidating, and my time and resources limited. To my regret, I had to set Bolivia aside, with the hope of picking it up again in other research in the not-too-distant future.

This book is based on fifteen years of work and hundreds of interviews with the various stakeholders involved in these local conflicts. The information I gathered during all those years was double-checked through in-depth desk research. I meticulously analyzed the dynamics that characterized each of the fifty-five local conflicts in the three countries I studied. Instead of developing a new theory of conflict, I seek to contribute analysis that can be useful to governments, investors, corporations, academics, and others involved in the oil and gas industry and to aid their efforts to minimize the risk of local conflicts. The book identifies possible policies and interventions that may help to reduce hydrocarbons-related conflicts, and it does so by analyzing in detail the dynamics, the actors, and the local context in which oil and gas disputes develop. I present this in-depth analysis in the form of an educated discussion of the causes and dynamics of local natural resource conflicts. I hope my findings will shed some light on why and how local oil-related conflicts develop and what can be done to reduce their numbers.

One of the main findings of the book is that while hydrocarbons conflicts ranging across countries and regions have similar causes and effects, each case should be analyzed with attention to its very specific context. Investigations should delve into the particular sociopolitical and economic scenario of each conflict, the nature of the stakeholders involved, and the history of past disputes in the area, among other factors. It is primarily these particular and very contextual dynamics of the dispute that need to be addressed to reduce the risk of violence.

An underlying message of the book is that resolving these local conflicts will require a strong political commitment that goes beyond ensuring that oil and gas revenues are distributed in an equitable way. The society as a whole will need to find a balance between obtaining the economic benefits of oil and gas development and addressing its social and environmental costs. This is not an easy task, and it will call for a thorough understanding of the triggers of local oil conflicts, particularly when communities with diverse cultures, such as Indigenous Peoples, are involved.

Oftentimes, there is not a visible trigger, but problems arise from the perception by the local community of potential danger associated with the oil project. This perception may originate from a previous negative experience of the affected community or from information about oil-related problems in nearby areas. I have seen government authorities often wonder how communities can reject an oil project even before it starts and why they assume it will be bad for them. Understanding the background behind that rejection and its general context could perhaps help to minimize, or even prevent, a conflict. When Indigenous communities are involved, it is particularly important to understand how perceptions are influenced by particular cultural, historical, and social characteristics.

I am profoundly indebted to the hundreds of Latin Americans in cities and in remote areas across the region who confided their views, feelings, thoughts, and fears to me. It is thanks to them that I was able to start piecing this book together. Thanks are also due to my friends and colleagues who believed in my project even before I did and who helped me get where I wanted to go. I am particularly grateful to Hector Torres, Karen Matusic, and Maurice Walsh for their generous words, which opened up the first doors toward this book.

I am thankful to the Institute of Peace for betting on my project when it was still an incipient idea. I am particularly grateful to my colleagues at the Jennings Randolph Fellowship Program, Chantal de Jonge Oudraat, Elizabeth "Lili" Cole, and Virginia "Ginny" Bouvier, for their constant support and patience; to Shira Lowinger and Janene Sawers for making things happen; to Tara Sonenshine for trusting in my project; and to many others who contributed to nurturing the right atmosphere for me to be creative and productive. Thank you all very much. I also thank Marc Sommers for putting me in touch with Nancy Grayson from the University of Georgia Press, who saw a book in my manuscript.

In Washington, D.C., I especially thank Robert Wasserstrom for his multiple, generous comments; Andrew Miller for his insight; and Jeff Pugh and Matt Finer for their help during the early stages of the project. My thanks also go to Melanie Bittle and Camilo Zambrano for all their effort in helping me with the early tedious work of piecing together the history of the case studies in each of the three countries I chose to examine. The matrixes they produced, with every single detail of each conflict, and the lively weekly discussions we had on their findings were a fundamental contribution to my analyses. I would also like to thank Sandra Polaski for her help with polishing my English and Andres Castello for his research efforts.

Finally, I probably would have not engaged in this project had it not been for the faith that two very important persons in my life had in me, even when my own trust faded. My mother, Tina, nurtured my interest in the world and my love for people of all origins from an early age and held my hand through bumps of all sorts. Her unconditional love and her strength continue to guide me even now that she is no longer with us. She was not able to see this project come to life, but I am sure she is proud of it from whatever constellation she now watches over me. Lastly, I dedicate this book to my husband, Alexandre Marc, who lived through the ups and downs of this project, the frustrations and the victories, and whose thoughts, inspiration, support, and love were instrumental in making it happen.

INTRODUCTION

ON JUNE 5, 2009, at least thirty-two people were killed and hundreds injured when security forces clashed with Indigenous Peoples in the bloodiest social unrest Peru has experienced in recent history.[1] Some eight hundred Indigenous demonstrators took over oil and gas infrastructure, blocked access roads, and interrupted exports from the country's main oil production area, located in the Amazonian province of Bagua. The clashes followed seven weeks of street protests by some thirty thousand Indigenous Peoples opposing a series of new government decrees that facilitated the sale of the lands they lived on to oil, gas, and timber developments. Carrying spears, their naked torsos and faces painted, the protestors marched day and night along the area's dirt roads, chanting antigovernment slogans. They took over the local airport, which belongs to a foreign oil company that had promised two billion dollars in new investments in Peru's most prolific oil region.

Peru has been adamantly trying to increase its hydrocarbons production to meet domestic needs and reduce increasingly expensive imports. But the upheaval raised questions about the feasibility of boosting private oil and gas investments. News of Peru's deadly clashes shocked the world and was echoed by the main media outlets:

"Oil and Land Rights in Peru: Blood in the Jungle"
   Economist, June 11, 2009
"'Many Missing' after Peru Riots"
   BBC News, June 8, 2009
"9 Hostage Officers Killed at Peruvian Oil Facility"
   Simon Romero, *New York Times*, June 6, 2009
"The Wounded in Hospitals in the Bagua and Jaen Regions Go Up to 169."
   La República, June 5, 2009

After the clashes, Indigenous spokespeople accused members of the armed forces of opening fire from a helicopter against peaceful demonstrators. But the government denied that account and said the demonstrators were armed and defiant. A prominent leader and organizer of the Indigenous marches fled to exile in Nicaragua for fear of being detained in Peru. Human rights organizations around the world condemned the clashes and called on the government to reconsider its decision to pass the controversial decrees. A few days later, the president of Peru said the decrees would most likely be rescinded to open the way for a negotiating period with the Indigenous communities.

During a press conference following the deadly confrontations, Indigenous leaders said they would continue to oppose the decrees, which they feared would facilitate an invasion of their lands by foreign companies. They believe they should be consulted before any kind of industrial development is planned for their territories. The government, however, maintains that the fact that they were born there does not mean they own the natural resources of the area. In Peru the constitution states that the government is the legal administrator of subsoil natural resources and has the power to decide how and when to develop them, regardless of who is living on the surface.

Events similar to those in Bagua have been multiplying throughout Latin America, paralleling the unprecedented economic expansion that the region experienced in the first decade of the twenty-first century. Economic growth has come in response to high commodity prices, increased international demand, and overall sound investment policies. The strengthening of democratic governance throughout the region and the end of the Cold War has introduced Latin America to a more stable political environment than that which existed in the 1960s and 1970s. Political stability has contributed to the sound economic performance of the twenty-first century and has facilitated the arrival of new investments, particularly in natural resources. Oil exploration and hydrocarbons development projects have experienced a boom, mainly in the Amazon jungle, which holds largely undeveloped reserves.[2]

Parallel to the obvious economic benefits of this hydrocarbons boom and to the generalized optimism it has generated came a dramatic increase in the number of conflicts related to the new projects. Conflicts have been especially serious in the Amazon, which is home to large numbers of Indigenous and farming populations whose attitude toward the new developments has been generally hostile. The rapid expansion of bloody conflicts at times has threatened the relative social peace that has prevailed in Latin America since the end of the 1980s. The increased violence has also thrown into question the sustainability of long-term economic growth for the region, particularly growth based on natural resources.

Oil and gas conflicts often feed on the social and economic frustrations of the population affected by them, usually Indigenous Peoples, who feel they are being once again excluded from the benefits of economic development enjoyed by the rest of society. A new feeling of empowerment among local Indigenous communities, derived from an expanded national and international recognition of their political and economic marginalization, has contributed to their growing militancy. Indigenous groups have a strong impetus for defending their territories from new and expanding oil and gas developments when they feel they are not sharing in the benefits. The fight for recognition of the rights of Indigenous populations is at the heart of local hydrocarbons conflicts, which are rapidly becoming a new platform for social mobilization in Latin America.

This book provides an analysis of the elements that contribute to the development of local oil- and gas-related conflicts in Latin America, their nature and dynamics, and the reasons for their proliferation. It also looks at the factors and actions that may help prevent such conflicts—or at least mitigate their intensity. Unlike previous work regarding natural resources and conflict, this study explores nonarmed conflict situations, particularly at the community level, rather than armed confrontations and civil wars.[3] The book provides suggestions for the incorporation of dispute resolution mechanisms in relation to oil and natural gas developments. These recommendations are based on an in-depth analysis of the year-by-year development of dozens of conflicts in Peru, Ecuador, and Colombia and on concrete, practical findings.

Conflicts over natural resources are not new to the region. Throughout its history Latin America has witnessed numerous disputes that could be classified within four broad categories: geopolitical troubles, border issues, revenue distribution, and local differences over the development of natural resources (Vasquez 2011, 12–16). Many of the conflicts that characterized the Cold War period were geopolitically driven. These types of conflicts typically involved the use of oil or gas for building cross-country alliances, with the goal of imposing specific political or ideological changes. The best recent example of a geopolitical conflict in Latin America involves Venezuela during the administration of President Hugo Chávez, who used his country's ample oil and gas reserves—80.5 billion barrels of proven oil and 149 trillion cubic feet of natural gas—to craft energy cooperation programs with ideological allies. The Petrocaribe Initiative, created in 2005, supported political alliances by guaranteeing Venezuelan oil at preferential prices to Caribbean countries, and through the Bolivarian Alliance for the Americas, Caracas contributed to the development of energy projects in politically friendly countries.[4] By contrast, governments not aligned with President Chávez's political views live with the specter of supply interruptions by Caracas. A strong critic of the United States, Chávez put his country's natural gas trade with neighboring Colombia at stake in 2009, as a result of Bogota's decision to step up the presence of U.S. military forces in its territory. Chávez raised the possibility of shutting down the 224-kilometer Trans-Caribbean gas pipeline that connects Colombia's Ballena field with Venezuela's oil-producing Maracaibo region. In the end, the threats failed to materialize into concrete action. Such ideologically driven interstate conflict has become more sporadic around the world since the 1989 fall of the Berlin wall, and Latin America is part of that trend. The geopolitical conflicts around natural resources that prevail in Latin America today no longer pose a real threat to the relatively young regional democracies, with the possible exception of Venezuela's use of its oil resources as a political pressure tool.

The second type of hydrocarbons dispute between states is linked to border conflicts, which are also less frequent nowadays in Latin America. Newly emerging border disputes around oil or gas are usually addressed through diplomatic channels, even if they may still trigger deep hostility among the countries involved. The resolution of hydrocarbons differences through war was a reality of the past century. In 1932, for example, Bolivia began three years of bloody armed confrontation with Paraguay over control of the Chaco boreal region, which was mistakenly thought to contain large reserves of oil. By contrast, a more recent border dispute between Peru and Chile was resolved peacefully, if not necessarily in an economically sound manner. In 2005 Peru unilaterally redrew its maritime boundaries with Chile, altering a bilateral agreement signed fifty years earlier. In response, Santiago gave up its previous decision to buy Peruvian gas to make up for dwindling imports from Argentina (Vasquez 2005). Instead, Chile decided to import liquefied natural gas from international markets, a more expensive option, but one that guaranteed regular supplies and shielded Santiago from potential future border conflicts with Peru.

Probably the most damaging historical border conflict, with long-lasting violent effects even in modern-day Latin America, was the 1880s War of the Pacific between Chile and Bolivia. During that confrontation Chile took away Bolivia's access to the Pacific Ocean and left it landlocked, planting the seeds of a Bolivian antagonism toward Chileans that is still very much alive. That deeprooted feeling was externalized in 2002 with the start of the deadly events that became known as the "Gas Wars." Popular opposition in Bolivia to government proposals for exporting landlocked Bolivian natural gas through a Chilean port triggered violent street confrontations that left dozens dead and contributed to the ousting of two Bolivian presidents—Gonzalo Sanchez de Lozada in 2003, and his successor, Carlos Mesa, in 2005. Thus the initiative to export Bolivia's gas to the United States and Mexico through a port in Chile fell through, as the private consortium leading the export project decided to set up operations in Peru instead.

The third type of conflict—related to the distribution of revenues—occurs within a country's borders and is well illustrated by the case of Bolivia, following the discovery of an estimated 9.9 trillion cubic feet of proven natural gas reserves (EIA 2012a). A long-term struggle was set in motion among various Bolivian regions for control of the new gas revenues in a confrontation charged with strong ethnic overtones. The relatively small percentage of the population of Spanish descent, who control the gas-producing southeastern provinces of Tarija, Santa Cruz, and Cochabamba, confronted the majority of the country's population of Indigenous ancestry. Behind the ethnic element were class differences that have been historically manifested in deep economic and social inequalities between the two groups, with the majority Indigenous Peoples, who live mainly in the highlands, experiencing higher poverty rates than the rest of the population.

With the ascendancy to power of Indigenous President Evo Morales in 2006, Bolivia's majority Indigenous population held political power for the first time. Upon taking office, Morales was immediately confronted with calls for autonomy by the gas-rich states, for fear they would lose control of the profitable gas reserves to the majority population of Indigenous descent. Defying the opposition from the lowlands, the new president set out to redistribute gas revenues in the form of new social programs and to rewrite the constitution to increase the rights and political representation of the majority Indigenous population. His efforts were met with bloody demonstrations, as pro- and antigovernment protesters clashed over gas revenue distribution.

The last type of dispute related to the development of hydrocarbons—local conflicts—is the main focus of this book. For the past two decades, this has been Latin America's fastest growing category of conflicts in relation to oil and gas development, but the least studied. The negative environmental and social externalities brought about by the boom in the exploration and development of hydrocarbons reserves, and the impact these have had on local communities, constitute the main trigger of local conflicts today. Local conflicts are geographically limited to the boundaries of the oil or gas project that originally sparks them, and they involve Indigenous Peoples, and sometimes farming communities living in the area. Underlying these dynamics are old, unresolved grievances and a history of marginalization of the affected groups. As illustrated by the Bagua events, if not addressed properly and in a timely fashion, local conflicts can have regional—and sometimes even nationwide—impacts. Their rapid proliferation and increasingly violent nature threaten the sustainability of Latin America's natural resource-based economic growth.

The knot of elements that characterize local conflicts is not easy to untie. First, a large number of very different stakeholders represents many interlaced and sometimes opposed interests. Among the main actors are various levels of government bureaucracies that are often not coordinated with one another; Indigenous Peoples, who are protected by specific laws; a variety of nongovernmental and international organizations that represent the interests of local groups; environmental nongovernmental organizations (NGOs) that advocate mainly an ecological agenda in relation to oil projects; and the oil companies responsible for developing the oil and gas reserves.

Second, more often than not the laws available to solve local conflicts are not clear or properly interpreted, and they are sometimes wrongly implemented, overlapping, or contradictory. Third, oil companies contribute their share to local conflicts by not always adopting sound social and environmental standards. Fourth, weak governance, corruption, and nontransparent rules at subnational government levels often lead to inequitable allocation of new oil revenues and eventually to conflict.

This book focuses on hydrocarbons-related local conflicts in Colombia, Peru, and Ecuador, where the number of new oil and gas projects has increased the most in the past two decades, particularly in remote Amazon territories inhabited by Indigenous and farming populations. In the presence of an external challenge—such as an oil project—the deep ethnic identity that characterizes Indigenous populations becomes a key unifying element and a channel for the expression of economic, social, political, and cultural grievances, in a way that sometimes results in conflict (Stewart 2008, 3–25).

These vulnerable groups have historically been the most affected by Latin America's deep-rooted social and economic inequalities. Nearly all countries in the region experience large disparities in income and access to basic services, education, and land tenure, among other variables. This is in spite of the notable economic growth of the past two decades, which resulted in a significant drop in poverty levels among Latin America's overall population: poverty rates dropped from 50 percent in 1990 to 32 percent in 2010 (ECLAC 2010b).

While the bulk of the oil and gas resources in Peru and Ecuador are in the Amazon basin, in Colombia most of the traditional oil production is concentrated in adjacent areas—the eastern Llanos and Magdalena basins—which are not large enclaves of Indigenous populations. However, as hydrocarbons projects expand throughout the country, new oil areas in the southern Amazon department of Putumayo and the northern departments of Santander, Norte de Santander, and Boyaca, on the border with Venezuela, overlap with Indigenous populations.[5] Most important, Colombia's longest, still unresolved oil conflict involves the U'wa Indigenous population, which has opposed oil developments in its territory for fifteen years.

In the process of writing this book, I have been frequently asked why I didn't use Venezuela as a case study. The answer is one of dynamics and challenges. Historically, the oil industry has been the core around which Venezuela's economic, political, and even social dynamics of the past eighty years have played out. Oil developments and Venezuelan politics could be said to be a composite that responds in tandem to national and international stimuli. But in Venezuela today oil-related conflicts are mostly geopolitical, with the exception of a few border disputes, mainly related to the delimitation of natural gas areas bordering with neighboring Trinidad. Local conflicts resulting from oil operations are few and do not pose comparable democratic challenges as in other hydrocarbons-producing countries, mostly because new exploration has been limited and old producing areas are not large Indigenous enclaves.

Much of the research for this study was based on the analysis of human stories that developed around the oil and gas industries of Latin America and how they unfolded through the years. Interviews carried out with the different stakeholders through the years provided the elements for studying each case individually in order to be able to make educated assumptions. The identity of the majority of those interviewed has been kept anonymous as part of the journalistic ethic that calls for the protection of sources. A strict adherence to this golden rule of journalism contributed to gaining the trust of those interviewed, whose sometimes sensitive statements contributed to enriching this book. The primary information obtained was cross-examined among the different sources, across country borders, and with existing literature.

As part of the methodology used in this book, all available documented local conflicts around oil and gas projects in Peru, Ecuador, and Colombia between 1992 and 2010 are compiled in three matrices, one for each country. Each matrix includes chronological, detailed information about how the conflicts have developed, the elements that have contributed to their worsening and mitigation, and the interplay of the stakeholders. The meticulous analysis of every historical variable with a direct or indirect influence on the conflicts has been double-checked through interviews and literature research. A detailed description of each stage of the conflict throughout the years has allowed for an in-depth grasp of the dynamics at play in each case at each moment in time. Comparative analyses based on the mapping of fifty-five conflicts in each country has allowed for the formulation of initial conclusions that were subsequently verified.

The second phase of the methodology was to grade each stage of the local hydrocarbons conflicts on a scale from 0 to 5, reflecting various levels of intensity throughout their duration (see table 1). The highest grade indicates the maximum intensity reached by each conflict during the period under review.

Conflicts that resulted in full agreement after negotiations were graded "0," while disputes characterized by violent, nonauthorized actions that ended with major destruction or casualties received a "5."

Table 2 summarizes the number of conflicts that fall in the two highest levels of intensity (levels 4 and 5) in each of the three countries studied. Each conflict was analyzed throughout its duration and different actions or events were graded according to the scale specified in table 1.

Ecuador shows the highest number—ten—of level 5 disputes, the most violent type, almost half of this country's twenty-three conflicts. This may be due to the fact that conflicts are older in Ecuador than in the other two countries

---

TABLE 1   Scale of conflict intensity

HIGH intensity	5: Violent response with major destruction or casualties.
	4: Popular mobilizations and demonstrations.
MEDIUM intensity	3: Widely publicized disagreement leading to legal action.
	2: Publicly expressed disagreement, but with ongoing dialogue.
LOW intensity	1: Agreement reached, but slow implementation.
	0: Full settlement with satisfaction among all parties involved.

Source: Compiled by the author.

	High intensity conflicts		Total number of conflicts
Country	Level 5	Level 4	All levels
Ecuador	10	4	23
Peru	7	9	20
Colombia	7	1	12

TABLE 2   Number of conflicts per country

Source: Compiled by the author.

and have typically gone through various intensity levels throughout their duration. Once they reach the highest intensity it is probably a measure of last resort and proof that none of the previous steps offered much in the way of results for the affected communities. Peru and Colombia have fewer level 5 conflicts than Ecuador: a total of seven each. However, almost half of Colombia's twelve conflicts present a level 5 intensity, representing the same proportion of the total as Ecuador. In Peru level 5 conflicts represent roughly a third of a total of the twenty disputes. The persistence of high-intensity disputes in Colombia may be linked to the country's decades-old armed conflict, which tends to quickly escalate disputes into open violence and to directly influence local oil and gas conflicts. In Peru, level 4 conflicts represent a higher proportion of the total: nine out of twenty. This may be in part because conflicts are concentrated in a much shorter period. In contrast to Ecuador, Peru became a large natural gas producer only recently and has yet to find enough oil to become self-sufficient. Maybe due to that late start, Peru shows the fastest growing number of hydrocarbons-related conflicts in our study.

The book is divided into four chapters, plus an introduction and conclusion. The first two chapters set the sociopolitical and economic context in which hydrocarbons conflicts occur and include an overview of the historical developments that have contributed to the present conflictive situations. Chapter 1 offers an analysis of the trends that have shaped investor and government interest in oil and gas in Peru, Ecuador, and Colombia throughout the years. It particularly focuses on oil and gas in the Amazon region and presents an overview of the typology that characterizes hydrocarbons conflicts in Latin America. The second chapter analyzes the interrelationship between oil and gas projects in the Amazon and the local Indigenous population. This chapter presents the so-

cial, economic, and political dynamics of the Indigenous movement in the region and how these relate to hydrocarbons conflicts. Chapter 3 covers the structural flaws that fuel hydrocarbons conflicts and looks at issues such as the legal
frameworks, poor governance practices, and incomplete policies that have contributed to generating or aggravating conflicts. It uses the Peruvian example
of fiscal decentralization to represent subnational governance weaknesses that
have contributed to generating oil- and gas-related conflicts. Chapter 4 offers
an analysis of a series of stress factors that influence the intensity of the conflicts. Particular attention is given to the behavior of the various stakeholders
in intensifying or mitigating disputes. Chapter 4 also addresses in detail one of
the main messages of the book: the importance of well-respected institutions in
acting as mediators to resolve or mitigate hydrocarbons-related local conflicts.
Unfortunately, institution building is not one of Latin America's strengths. But
there are exceptions: examples of successful institutional intervention for mitigating local conflicts around oil or gas that can be good models to imitate. The
book particularly commends the Peruvian Office of the Ombudsman. Finally,
the conclusion offers a summary of the main findings and a few recommendations to prevent oil-related conflicts, or to contribute to reducing their intensity, in Latin America.

CHAPTER 1

Tracing Oil- and Gas-Related Conflicts

CONFLICTS AROUND hydrocarbons are not new in the three countries under study, and they can be traced back to the beginning of oil operations in Colombia at the beginning of the twentieth century. But it was not until the large oil discoveries of the 1970s and 1990s that the dynamics of the oil-related conflicts as we know them today started to develop, particularly in the western Amazon region. It was then that the discovery of large oil reserves turned Ecuador, Colombia, and Peru into oil and gas producers, and the first seeds of oil-related conflicts were planted in the region.

Since then, oil investments have come and gone throughout the years, in tandem with shifts in domestic oil policies and fiscal incentives and the international price of crude. Investor interest has become particularly strong in the past decade, when conventional world oil reserves started to dwindle and high international oil prices turned previously expensive unconventional Amazon oil into a more tangible option. The western Amazon suddenly took a prominent place in the oil and gas map of Latin America, and its share of world hydrocarbons is expected to continue to grow as world demand for oil and gas increases.

This chapter traces the historical development of the oil and gas industries in the three countries and the growing importance of western Amazon in that process. It analyzes Latin America's increasingly prominent stand in the world oil and gas scenario, evidenced by the current rapid growth of foreign direct investments in those sectors of the economy.

THE WORLD OIL AND GAS CONTEXT

The world map of oil and gas developments has changed dramatically in the past two decades. The Western Hemisphere has been taking a progressively significant role in the discovery of new reserves, and South American countries are among the leading forces behind that trend. Brazil is set to become a world oil superpower and to challenge Middle Eastern oil producers. Colombia's oil production has grown so fast during the past decade that the country managed to reverse a long tendency of output drop that threatened to turn it into a crude importer. And Peru became South America's first exporter of liquefied natural gas in 2010, while Argentina is third in the global ranking of countries with potentially large shale gas reserves, after China and the United States (EIA 2012b).

During the 1980s Mexico and the North Sea produced much of the world oil supplies outside the Middle East. But in the 1990s and the first decade of the twenty-first century, much of those crude supplies came instead from South America, China, and Middle Eastern countries that are not members of the Organization of Petroleum Exporting Countries (IEA 2010, 28).[1] With the end of the era of cheap and easy-to-find conventional oil and turmoil in the Middle East that threatened steady crude flows, companies started to look for new, largely unexplored areas holding nonconventional reservoirs, and South America quickly became a magnet.[2]

The increase in oil prices—from twenty-three U.S. dollars a barrel in 2001 to one hundred in May 2011—played a fundamental role in rapidly turning previously expensive hydrocarbons resources into more available options. Risky, unknown, and largely unexplored areas deep in the Amazon jungle became suddenly more attractive for investors. This tendency was further accelerated by China's—and to a lesser extent India's—growing hunger for imported fossil fuels to meet their burgeoning domestic energy demand. In terms of oil production, Latin America is expected to be the second-fastest-growing region (after North America) and will become increasingly well placed to meet the expected growing world demand of coming decades (IEA 2010, 78–93).

Worldwide demand for oil is expected to continue to grow in coming decades. China's oil demand could almost double by 2035, to 15.3 million barrels per day, from 8.1 million in 2009 (IEA 2010, 102). In 2009 China imported a total of 5.1 million barrels per day of oil, of which 14 percent—or 360,000—came from Latin America (BP 2010, 20). The International Energy Agency (2010, 78–193) predicts that in a hypothetical, and extreme, scenario of no new government policies for meeting energy or climate targets (such as those aimed at reducing greenhouse gas emissions), world demand for oil will shoot up to around 108 million barrels per day by 2035, from 85 million in 2009. Of that projected total demand, as much as 57 percent will come from China.

World demand for natural gas has followed a similar pattern of fast growth over the past two decades, and it will continue that trend for years to come.

Much as with oil, gas demand is expected to increase globally, but particularly in China, where it is projected to skyrocket from around 315 billion in 2009 to 14.1 trillion cubic feet in 2035 (IEA 2010, 180–81). Latin America is projected to provide 17 percent of that total world demand, up from 11 percent in 2008 (IEA 2010, 190–92). Gas will most likely overtake coal in the next two decades as the second fuel in the world energy mix after oil (IEA 2011, 19–22). More than half of that growth will be as liquefied natural gas, as trade in this form of gas will more than double to 17.6 trillion cubic feet by 2035 from 2008 figures. Trinidad and Tobago were the only exporters of liquefied natural gas in the region until 2010, when Peru followed suit from its giant Camisea field, located in the Amazon jungle (*Petroleum Economist* 2011).

OIL AWAKENING IN THE AMAZON

Outside of Venezuela, a significant part of Latin America's still-undeveloped and partly unexplored onshore gas and oil reserves are located in hard-to-reach areas of the Amazon jungle in Peru, Ecuador, and Colombia. There are also reserves in deep-sea waters off the coast. For the past two decades governments and investors have been increasingly focusing their attention in these areas to make up for the scarcity of conventional reserves around the world. High oil prices and increasing world demand suddenly made unconventional Amazon and deep-water areas more cost effective to develop.

Nine countries share the Amazon basin: Brazil, Bolivia, Colombia, Ecuador, Guyana, French Guyana, Peru, Surinam, and Venezuela, but most of it— around 68 percent—is in Brazil. The proportion of the Amazon basin in Peru, Ecuador, and Colombia is relatively small: 13 percent in Peru, 5.5 percent in Colombia, and 1.7 percent in Ecuador. But the basin acquires immense importance in proportion to the national territory of each of the countries: it expands across 75 percent of Peru, 45 percent of Ecuador, and 36 percent of Colombia (Fontaine 2007b). The eastern portion of the Amazon basin is located entirely in Brazil, while the western area extends across Colombia, Ecuador, Peru, and Bolivia.

In general, references to Amazon environmental threats are concerned with the eastern Brazilian portion, which has been traditionally characterized by high deforestation. In 2011 the eastern Brazilian Amazon was the focus of much local opposition to plans for building two hydroelectric projects—the Belo Monte Dam and the Madeira River Complex (Salazar-Lopez 2011). But much attention

The western Amazon (Finer et al. 2008).

has also focused on western Amazon, where there has been a considerable in-crease in the number of oil and gas licenses in the past decade, particularly in Peru, and to a lesser extent in Ecuador and Colombia. Peru granted eighty-six oil and gas licenses in 2010 (up from just twenty-eight in 2003), of which almost half—thirty-seven—are located in the Amazon. Scholars have documented that almost half of the Peruvian Amazon—48.6 percent—was covered with oil and gas concessions in 2007 (up from 7.1 percent in 2003), and by 2010 active and planned hydrocarbons developments expanded throughout 70 percent of the jungle in that country (Orta-Martinez and Finer 2010).

Initial oil exploration and production in the Amazon goes back to the 1900s and was limited to small quantities of crude produced in Peru. But the real oil boom started in the 1970s and spread throughout western Amazon. Many of the new oil exploration and development blocks there overlap with the territo-ries of largely forgotten and marginalized Indigenous or farming populations and have caused much disruption to their lives and to the local environment. Oil projects that build new access roads also bring colonization to previously remote forest areas, which results in increased logging, hunting, and deforestation (Finer et al. 2008).

Peru, Ecuador, and Colombia are generally referred to as Andean countries, because they share the Andes mountain range and some of the cultural characteristics linked to that area. But that definition neglects the fact that these three countries also share the Amazon and all the cultural and environmental distinctiveness associated with that region. When oil operations started to expand in the Amazon, local communities with shared cultural and territorial characteristics came together in opposition to them. Later on, we will analyze in detail the nature of the conflicts that emerged from that opposition in the Peruvian and Ecuadorean Amazon. We will also point out parallels and differences with oil conflicts in the non-Amazon producing areas of Colombia, where that country's largest crude reserves are located. In Colombia, oil operations at present occupy only 10 percent of the jungle, but they are rapidly expanding (Finer et al. 2008).

It is the Amazon that turned Ecuador and Peru into oil and gas producers in the 1970s. It is also in the Amazon that most of the social and environmental negative consequences of the expanding hydrocarbons industry are found. And it is there where the escalating number of hydrocarbons-related conflicts involving Indigenous communities occurs. This is not surprising, given Latin America's large Indigenous population and the widespread Indigenous inhabitance in the Amazon. Peru has the largest Indigenous population overall, of around 4.4 million (in a total Peruvian population of 27.5 million) (INDEPA 2010; Office of the Ombudsman, 2006).[3] The Peruvian Amazon is home to fifty-one ethnic groups (of a total of sixty around the country) that are organized in thirteen linguistic families and to fourteen or fifteen groups living in voluntary isolation (INDEPA 2010). Of Colombia's Indigenous population of a little over 1.37 million (3.4 percent of the country's total population), around 74 percent live in the Amazon: sixty-two Indigenous groups, of a total of eighty-three around the country (RAISG 2009; IWGIA 2010, 136; DANE 2005). In Ecuador almost 7 percent of the total population of some 14 million inhabitants are Indigenous and belong to twenty-nine different nationalities and pueblos (INEC 2001). Most of Ecuador's Indigenous population lives in the Amazon, including two groups living in voluntary isolation—Tagaeri and Taromenane—within the boundaries of Yasuni National Park, which is also home to the country's largest still-untapped hydrocarbons reserves. The broad intersection between Indigenous populations and hydrocarbons reserves at a time of high interest in oil and gas investments is at the core of many conflicts.

THE FIRST SPARKS

Oil and gas conflicts go back to the beginnings of oil operations, although the characteristics of the disputes have changed over time. During the first decades of the 1900s, conflicts were largely between the oil companies doing exploration work and governments or land-owning elites that kept much of the profits from the oil operations. The disputes were generally around the sharing of economic benefits from oil. For governments those benefits could take the form of loans or bribes or they could simply be arrangements with foreign oil companies that offered to facilitate access to international financing for local elites or politicians. In exchange, companies were given exceptional investment conditions and access to potential reserves. In Peru the International Petroleum Company was exempt from almost all taxes and had the monopoly on oil supply to the domestic market (Philip 1982, 21–31).

Border conflicts for control of areas rich in hydrocarbons were also common throughout the region. In 1941 Peru and Ecuador went to war over what some historians view as a dispute for the control of oil reserves, although others disagree (Martz 1987, 49–53). Before that there was the bloody Chaco War (1832–1935) between Bolivia and Paraguay for control of the Chaco Boreal.

It was not until the discovery of oil in the Amazon in the 1970s that local conflicts with the population living in the areas of exploration and production started. When oil companies arrived in the Amazon, the presence of the state there was extremely weak, as were policies for the economic or territorial development of the area and for the protection of its social and environmental patrimony. The presence of oil led to the creation of towns around the hydrocarbons activities, which in turn attracted an outside population in search of jobs. In Ecuador, for example, the arrival of Texaco to the Amazon region in the 1960s resulted in the creation of Lago Agrio, the capital of the province of Sucumbios, which later became a base for the company's operations. Roads were built to access the hydrocarbons-producing areas, facilitating the arrival of colonizers, exacerbating tensions with the local population, and planting the seeds for future resentment.

Historically, the sources of the oil conflicts that exist today may be traced back to the early 1900s in Colombia, in relation to that country's two initial oil concessions, Barco and De Mares. The opening up of lengthy expanses of territory for construction of two pipelines that would transport oil from the producing areas caused three types of local conflicts from early on: between the oil company and local inhabitants being displaced for construction of the pipelines, between local inhabitants and the newly arrived colonizers settling in the area and competing for oil jobs, and between oil workers (most of them newcomers) and the Tropical Oil Company, which operated the De Mares concession, for better living conditions. This last dispute had long-lasting historical consequences. What differentiated this conflict from others was that it involved a new actor: the workers' union. In 1922 an oil workers' union was created in Colombia to defend the rights of local inhabitants and oil workers, and after relentless activism and worker pressure it succeeded in obtaining the termination of the De Mares concession in 1951 and its takeover by the state (Avellaneda Cusaria 2004).[4] At that point, the state-owned oil company Ecopetrol was created by Law 165, and the country's oil industry entered a new era that would be characterized by stronger union activism and state control.

Colombia has been a pioneer in the adoption of conflict-mitigation mechanisms applied through practices of citizen participation. The 1991 constitutional reform began the development of the legal tools needed for these participatory procedures. Particularly noteworthy is Law NO. 850, passed in 2003, establishing citizen oversights (*veedurías ciudadanas* in Spanish), whose function is to supervise public and private expenditure and investments. Unfortunately, in several cases where citizen oversight was established for supervising the use of revenues in oil-producing departments, some of the participants were murdered and the participation process lost popularity (Quevedo 2007).

For the past forty years, a large number of oil disputes in Colombia have been connected to the country's long-term armed conflict. This is what distinguishes them from similar disputes in Peru and Ecuador. Typically, oil conflicts in Colombia may be of two types. One that is unique to that country today is characterized by armed groups taking illegal actions, such as the seizure of oil revenues, attacks against oil infrastructure, or the kidnapping of oil workers. A second type involves mainly Indigenous Peoples, and sometimes peasant communities, who, as in Peru and Ecuador, protest the disruption to their lives brought about by the development of hydrocarbons in their territories.

HOW IT ALL STARTED

The origins and later expansion of oil and gas development in Peru, Ecuador, and Colombia went hand in hand with the creation of the first large oil corporations by the nations that dominated the world political and economic scene at the end of the 1800s. Standard Oil in the United States, Royal Dutch Shell in

Europe, and later on British Petroleum Corporation in the United Kingdom, among others, were the pioneering designers of the global oil industry that was starting to emerge, and Latin America was already part of the oil map of the time (Yergin 1991, 20–164).

Oil exploration in the three countries started in the late 1800s and continued until the beginning of the twentieth century, but at relatively low levels. Commercial oil production in quantities large enough to make real profits on the market did not start until decades later. Initial oil discoveries in Peru and Ecuador were made on the Pacific coast, far from the Amazon reserves that would turn both countries into hydrocarbons exporters. When asked about the history of oil production in their country, Peruvians proudly say that northern Peru was the site of the second oil well in the Western Hemisphere, following oil man Edwin Drake's drilling of the first one in Titusville, Pennsylvania, in 1859. A few years later, the first geological oil mapping was carried out in Peru's northwestern coastal tip, with positive results.

Peru's oil production expanded greatly between the 1890s and the 1930s, mainly from three fields: Negritos, Lobitos, and Zorritos, located in the northwestern Piura region.[5] A smaller field, Pirin, had been discovered in 1875 in the southeastern department of Puno, in the Altiplano, but it soon dried out. During that time, Peru became an oil exporter, with only 10 percent of the production consumed internally. Oil production was mainly in the hands of foreign companies that exported the crude from their own ports, located close to the fields, on the northern coast. The oil operators of the time held production contracts for unlimited periods in exchange for a tax payment (Thorp and Bertram 1978, 95–111). By 1949 one foreign company, the International Petroleum Company, a subsidiary of Standard Oil of New Jersey, controlled 80 percent of Peru's petroleum output and to a large extent the country's economy (U.S. Senate 1952, 21–36). The company managed to guarantee its monopoly power over Peru's oil industry by establishing itself as the facilitator of short-term loans to successive governments, which it could easily obtain given its international reputation and connections: the company arranged for Peru to borrow five million U.S. dollars in 1946 and ten million in 1953 (Philip 1982, 243–57).

As in Peru, Ecuador's first oil reserves were discovered on the Pacific coast, in the Santa Elena Peninsula, but they were not large enough to be commercially viable. There, Anglo Ecuadorean Oilfields (an affiliate of the British Anglo Persian Oil that later became British Petroleum) started exploration works in 1918 and produced small amounts—around twelve hundred barrels per day—

for export. Exploration in the oil-rich Oriente region started three years later with the arrival of the Leonard Exploration Company from New York (later Standard Oil), which obtained a fifty-year concession, which was soon canceled. Following passage of the Petroleum Law of 1937, Anglo Saxon Petroleum (then owned by Royal Dutch Shell) received an oil concession in the Amazon Oriente to explore a vast area of ten million hectares (Martz 1987, 45–48). Between 1937 and 1942 the company drilled the first wells in an area known as Villano, which years later would acquire international notoriety for a long-lasting conflict with the Sarayaku Indigenous group living there.

Colombia's first two oil discoveries also coincided with the start of the 1900s. One was in the northeast region of Catacumbos, located in the department of Norte de Santander, close to the Venezuelan border. There, the Barco concession development began in 1913, first by Gulf Oil and then by Texas Mobil. The second oil development was in the Middle Magdalena River valley, under the De Mares concession, which was in the hands of Tropical Oil Company (colloquially known as Troco).

Initially, foreign oil companies that operated in Ecuador and Peru signed concession contracts that allowed them to develop and commercialize crude in a specific area for an agreed-on period in exchange for a royalty payment. Those rules changed in the 1950s, when the state assumed a more prominent role in the oil industry in both countries. At that point, concession contracts were replaced with participation and association agreements with state-owned oil companies. In Colombia the transfer of the De Mares concession to Ecopetrol in 1951 was part of that regional trend.

By 1969 Colombia had nationalized its oil resources with passage of Law 20, which introduced association contracts between the state and foreign companies. Under these contracts state-owned Ecopetrol received not only royalties but also part of the production, for being a partner in a consortium with private companies. A legal modification introduced in 1994 increased the state's share of production revenues even more, from 50 percent to as much as 75 percent, once investments and costs were recovered, or when production exceeded sixty million barrels. By comparison, Ecuador's state share of oil revenues in the 1900s was 62 percent, through state-owned oil company Petroecuador. In Peru the expropriation of the International Petroleum Company's assets in 1968 marked a turning point toward full-fledged nationalization. At that time, anti-U.S. sentiment was growing in Lima, and the company received no compensation, which led to serious political frictions between the two countries.

Like no other commodity, oil awakens strong nationalistic sentiments. This was true in the early days of production and continues to be so through the twentieth and twenty-first centuries. Originally, the debate around hydrocarbons developments was heavily polarized between those who rejected the presence of foreign multinationals and those who thought they were essential, because governments lacked the know-how and the capital necessary to develop the national oil industry. These opposed points of view resulted in constant policy shifts throughout the history of each country's oil development from pro-state to investor-friendly approaches, depending on which side held power at a given time. This political back and forth is one of the factors that continues to shape oil policies even today.

BLACK GOLD BECOMES A REALITY

The discovery of large, commercially valuable oil and gas reserves between the 1970s and the 1990s modified the dynamics of the three countries forever. Ecuador and Peru became major oil and gas producers, thanks to the discovery of the Amazon fields, and Colombia turned into one of Latin America's main oil producers following the discovery of three major fields in the eastern region of the country.

Ecuador

Amazon oil from Lago Agrio (also known as Nueva Loja), in the province of Sucumbios, turned a page in Ecuador's history. By 1972 Ecuador became a crude exporter, and oil became key for Quito's political, economic, and social dynamics for years to come. State-owned oil company Corporación Estatal de Petróleos de Ecuador (CEPE) was created in 1972, and Ecuador joined OPEC the following year.[6]

The oil boom of the 1970s hit Ecuador so suddenly that there was not enough time to build much oil expertise, and decisions on contracts, oil policies, and legislation needed to be adopted quickly (Martz 1987, 43–63). It was widely accepted that the new oil wealth would bring about important improvements in the country's political, economic, and social life, and the government wanted to be in control of that process. So by 1976 CEPE became the de facto main shareholder of the Texaco concession in Lago Agrio. Texas-Gulf was forced to hand over more than 60 percent of its share to the government and was allowed to keep the rest until 1992, when Petroecuador (successor of CEPE) took full control (Philip 1982, 274–80).

The Law of Hydrocarbons was reformed in 1993 by Law 44 (R. O. 326, 29-XI-1993) to increase the role of Petroecuador in upstream operations while at the same time going in the opposite direction in downstream operations (refining, transportation, and commercialization), where foreign investments were welcomed. This move reversed twenty years of state domination in downstream operations and had a very specific goal: to amass the necessary funds to double oil transportation capacity, which had become a bottleneck to increased production. The hope was that by updating and doubling transportation capacity, Ecuador would be able to also double its oil production.

Crude was until then transported from the Amazon fields through the 310-mile-long Sistema de Oleoducto TransEcuatoreano network, which had a transport capacity ceiling of 390,000 barrels per day and was controlled by Petroecuador. In response to calls for expanding oil transport infrastructure, a second, almost parallel oil pipeline came onstream in 2003. The 450,000 barrels per day capacity of Oleoducto de Crudos Pesados (OCP) was managed by private companies and stretched across the country, from the Amazon fields in the east to the Pacific Ocean in the west.

By some accounts, the 300-mile-long OCP was built in preparation for the future development of the fields in Ishpingo, Tambococha, and Tiputini (ITT), in Yasuni National Park, which had caught the eye of oil investors early on. The ITT fields hold Ecuador's most promising undeveloped crude reserves, estimated at one billion barrels, or the equivalent of almost 15 percent of the country's total reserves (Andrade Echeverría 2010, 104–5). But development of the full capacity of the ITT fields has been delayed due to much opposition, given its potential negative social and environmental effects. Home to various Indigenous groups, Yasuni National Park is one of the most unique biodiversity regions of the western Amazon.

The truth is that transportation through the OCP has always remained below capacity because private investors have been reluctant to make new commitments to boost Ecuador's output. Political instability, unclear and constantly changing rules of the game, and barriers to the development of the ITT fields created an atmosphere that was not conducive to renewed private interest. State-owned oil production was not any better. Petroecuador's weak financial situation prevented the company from either maintaining output constant in mature fields or expanding exploration to new areas. Service contractors accused Petroecuador of being in arrears in its payments and stopped providing services to the state company, while oil workers went on frequent strikes, all of which contributed to a decline in state oil production: Petroecuador went from producing roughly 110,000 barrels per day in 1995 to 70,000 in 2005 (Banco Central 2005, 47–48). Ecuador's dream of doubling output following construction of the OCP was further away than ever.

The lack of investor interest continued through the first decade of the twenty-first century, mainly driven by somewhat erratic oil policies, characterized by increased state control at a time when Peru and Colombia were going out of the way to attract hydrocarbons investments. With the arrival of President Rafael Correa in Ecuador in 2007, and his reelection in 2009, the investment atmosphere deteriorated even further. Companies were asked to renegotiate their contracts with the government and, after three years of seemingly unending negotiations, were forced to accept less profitable terms. In addition, a new hydrocarbons law, the Law to Reform the Hydrocarbons Law and the Tax Regime Law (R. O. 244), passed in 2010 increased the role of Petroecuador in crude developments.

Four companies—Brazilian Petrobras, China National Petroleum Company, South Korea's Canada Grande, and U.S.-based Energy Development Corporation—left the country over disagreements with the new terms the government wanted to impose on them, and Petroecuador took over their oil blocks (*El Comercio.com* 2010). A new state-owned oil company, Petroamazonas, was created to operate the fields taken away from the private operators.

The departure of the private oil companies came soon after the shock caused by the takeover of Block 15 from its operator, U.S. oil company Occidental. The government of Ecuador accused Oxy of breaking its contractual obligations by handing over a stake in that project to another firm without first consulting the authorities. Oxy took the case to arbitration at the World Bank's International Center for Settlement of Investment Disputes, an international tribunal frequently used by foreign oil companies to resolve disagreements with their host countries. Block 15 was very important for Ecuador because it was the country's largest privately operated field and was producing a significant one hundred thousand barrels per day when Petroecuador took it over in 2006. Around the same time, Petroecuador also seized the fields of another company, Perenco from France, due to tax disputes. A more restricted investor atmosphere resulted in large investment cutbacks, which in turn led to a striking 9 percent drop in total crude output between 2006 and 2009. From then on, investments

GRAPH 1   Ecuador: Oil production

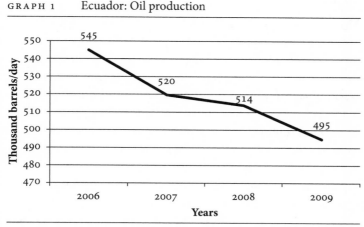

Source: Compiled by the author with data from BP (2011).

by companies that remained in Ecuador dropped by 23.8 percent, as they adopted a cautious approach, given the drastic changes in the country's investment scenario (Banco Central 2011; see graph 1).

The takeover of private output increased Petroecuador's oil portfolio, but the company failed to keep up with the newly acquired private production. Output from Block 15 alone dropped to 92,100 barrels per day only a year after its takeover, mainly due to inefficient management. Of the US$220.7 million budget Petroecuador had assigned to the field during 2006, only US$86.7 million, or less than 40 percent, was invested (Banco Central 2006). Two years later, two new discoveries—in the Drago field and the old Shushufindi field located in the Amazonian province of Sucumbios—changed the tide (Gill 2011). Output by Petroecuador and its subsidiary, Petroamazonas, recovered only slightly: from 466,000 barrels per day in January 2010 to 504,000 a year later. But reserves were positively impacted by the new finds and increased considerably in 2008 and 2009 to 6.5 billion barrels, from 4 billion registered in 2007 (Banco Central 2011).

Holding the third largest oil reserves in the region after Venezuela and Brazil, Ecuador is the fifth South American producer after Brazil, Venezuela, Argentina, and Colombia. Petroecuador has long been known for being notoriously dysfunctional, and corruption scandals within the company have been the standard rather than the exception throughout the history of the company. This trend probably signals overall mismanagement of the country's oil industry, which is the number one source of government revenues and accounts for 15 percent of the country's gross domestic product and 50 percent of its exports.

In the midst of various company scandals, President Correa was planning major reforms of Petroecuador and Petroamazonas at the time this book was being written (Ministry of Nonrenewable Resources 2011b). In September 2010 around 10 percent of Petroecuador's workforce was suspended under the suspicion that they were shareholders of another company that had been awarded fuel commercialization contracts and was planning to invest the proceeds in tourism projects. Ecuadorean law forbids state companies from entering into agreements that benefit their employees directly.

Under the Correa administration, much of Ecuador's new infrastructure investment was being financed with loans from China in exchange for future payment in barrels of Ecuadorean oil (Alvaro 2009). According to officials representing Chinese interests in the United States, China prefers these types of money-for-barrel arrangements to access Ecuadorean oil rather than entering into more formal contractual long-term exploration and development agreements. Chinese mistrust of the nontransparent and largely corrupt manner in which Ecuador has historically been known to manage its oil industry seems to be behind China's reasoning.

In 2010 two Chinese companies operating in Ecuador—Andes Petroleum and Petrooriental—made public their concerns about the lack of transparency during new contract negotiations and alleged that the government had tried to pressure them into accepting new, less advantageous contractual terms. Both Chinese companies threatened to seek international arbitration (Reuters 2010). To avoid this kind of retaliation by companies in the future, under the terms of the 2010 reforms to the hydrocarbons law, the government of Ecuador formally exited the International Center for Settlement of Investment Disputes.

Colombia

Colombia has the most successful oil industry of the three countries under study in this book. Oil in commercially viable quantities came to light in the 1980s and 1990s, with the discovery of three oil fields in the eastern region of the country. Caño Limón was discovered in the department of Arauca in 1984, and Cusiana and Cupiagua, located in the adjacent Casanare department, were discovered in 1986 and 1993, respectively. These oil finds turned the country into a significant oil producer and changed the demographic configuration of producing areas, as numerous peasants started to arrive in search of employment opportunities in the oil industry and mingled with Indigenous groups already living in the region. The new oil discoveries also attracted private investor interest in Colombia, in spite of relatively unfavorable contractual terms at the time. Colombia had become an oil exporter in 1969, and since then hydrocarbon laws had fluctuated from supporting private investments to moments of strong state control.[7]

The new discoveries of the 1980s and 1990s boosted oil production, but by the start of the year 2000 output started to decline at alarming rates. By 2004 oil production had fallen to 551,000 barrels per day from a peak of 800,000 in 1999, and there were fears that unless the falling trend was reversed, Colombia would soon cease to be one of South America's main crude producers and become an oil importer. Oil reserves also fell dramatically to 1.5 million barrels in 2004, from 2.3 million in 1999.

There were various reasons for the drastic drop in oil production. First, fields naturally declined, and there had not been major new reserves discoveries for some time. Second, frequent guerrilla attacks against oil infrastructure and the kidnapping of oil workers contributed to investors' losing interest in Colombia. Third, Colombia's challenging geology for the development of oil reservoirs has historically made that country's oil reserves more costly and riskier to develop than some of its regional neighbors, particularly oil-rich Venezuela.

The government was set on changing the tide by attracting private investments that would help reverse the worrisome decline of oil production and reserves. Faced with the prospect of Colombia becoming an oil importer, the government of President Alvaro Uribe (2002–10) launched investor-friendly changes to the regulatory framework and took measures to improve the security of oil infrastructure. The new regulations included royalties as low as 5 percent and the possibility for private investors to keep 100 percent of production in some cases. Also, the privatization of 20 percent of state-owned Ecopetrol was set in motion, and the Agencia Nacional de Hidrocarburos was created to oversee the development of the oil sector.[8]

The agency organized seven oil bidding rounds between 2007 and 2010, offering previously undeveloped regions in an effort to expand the hydrocarbons map. It succeeded in attracting new players to new areas located along the Pacific coast (onshore and offshore), in the southwestern Amazonian Putumayo department, and in the northern Caribbean, expanding the country's submarine platform. Under the new investment terms introduced in 2003, the most common oil contracts became associations between Ecopetrol and private investors, in which the state share could fluctuate between 30 percent and 60 percent.

By 2009 investment in the oil sector had risen to roughly US$2.5 billion, compared with negative figures in 1999 and 2000, and production had rebounded slightly to 685,000 barrels per day (Asociación 2013). Key to the attraction of new investment to the hydrocarbons sector was the introduction in 2005 of the Law of Judicial Stability for Investors in Colombia (no. 963), to guarantee that the terms and conditions of the investment would not be amended throughout the life of the project. By 2011 oil production had greatly recovered and at 916,000 barrels per day had surpassed peak 1999 levels. Oil reserves also went up to an estimated 2.3 million barrels (see graph 2). For Colombia, what mattered most was that new investment helped to stop a dangerous downward spiral of oil reserves and production that would have otherwise doomed the country's oil industry for decades to come.

According to the government, the oil industry restructuring greatly improved the rate of success of oil exploration, which went from just 21 percent of all wells drilled in 2003 to 67 percent in 2009 (Vera Díaz 2010). The bulk of Colombia's traditional oil production is mainly concentrated in areas spread out throughout three departments to the northeast—the old producing areas of Casanare and Arauca and a new production site in Meta—while natural gas

GRAPH 2   Colombia: Oil production

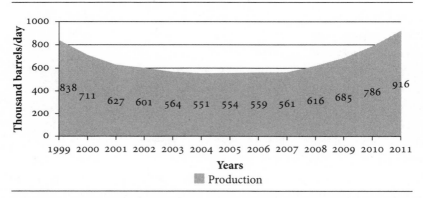

Source: Compiled by the author with data from BP (2011) and the Ministry of Mines and Energy of Colombia (1999–2011).

is mainly produced in the northern La Guajira department and to a lesser extent in Casanare. As investments started to make their way back to the country in the past decade, traditional oil regions expanded and new departments were added to the oil map. Colombia consumes around 280,000 barrels per day and exports the rest, mainly to the United States.

Peru

The case of Peru is somewhat different from the other two, because despite the fact that it is a major natural gas producer, it has still not discovered large oil reserves and is not yet self-sufficient in supplies of crude. Peru imports oil to meet its domestic needs, which results in significant trade deficits. In the 1990s Peru decided to reverse this situation, doing everything possible to rapidly develop its oil industry. A new law passed in 1993, the Law to Regulate Hydrocarbons Activities in the National Territory (no. 26221), provided the appropriate legal framework for attracting foreign companies through competitive contracts.

State-owned oil company Petroperu, created in 1969 by Decree 17753, kept control of a small portion of downstream operations, a few upstream assets, refining operations, gasoline stations, and the Transandean pipeline from the International Petroleum Corporation. But the bulk of the upstream industry was privatized, marking the beginning of a new era for the country's hydrocarbons industry, with the private sector taking a leading role in the industry (Mayorga Alba 2006, 387–407). A new government agency, Perupetro, created in 1993 by article 6 of Law 26221, promoted hydrocarbons investments and oversaw contract implementation.

This regulatory restructuring of the oil industry immediately caught the attention of foreign companies, and oil investments rose significantly, from US$19.89 million in 1993 to US$187 million in 1997, particularly in the tropical forests of the northern regions. The operational outcome of these efforts was not impressive, however, because no major oil reservoirs were found, and private interest consequently dropped. Investments in oil subsequently fell to less than US$13 million in 2000 (Ministry of Energy 1999, 2008), and as a result by 2003 oil production was at 92,000 barrels per day, down from 116,000 in 1998 (BP 2009). Oil reserves also greatly suffered from the lack of private investor interest and drastically dropped from 800 million barrels at the beginning of the 1990s to an average of 300 million barrels toward the end of that decade and the beginning of the next.

With little new oil to be found, and an expanding economy, Peru was forced to import crude to meet its domestic demands just when oil prices started to go up. To counter this situation, starting in 2004 the government launched a second aggressive oil exploration plan that included the development of marginal oil deposits and new fields throughout the country, including much of the Amazon region. By that time, the giant Camisea natural gas reserves that had been discovered in the Amazon in 1989 had started to produce and would soon turn Peru into South America's leading natural gas producer. Output from Camisea increased extraordinarily, from 36 million cubic feet per day in 2001 to more than one billion in 2011. In 2010 Peru became South America's first liquefied natural gas exporter (see graph 3).

With Camisea, Peru acquired for the first time a prominent place among the region's large energy producers and its main exporters. The giant gas reserves, which were managed by a private consortium, also helped to attract investor interest in the Andean country's overall energy potential. The investor-friendly policies introduced in 2004 led to a sharp recovery in oil investment, which went from US$160 million in 1999 to US$1.5 billion in 2008. Especially attractive to investors were royalty rates as low as 5 percent and the introduction in 2007 of a new system of competitive bidding. The restructuring abandoned the one-on-one negotiations between Perupetro and selected oil operators, which

GRAPH 3   Peru: Natural gas production

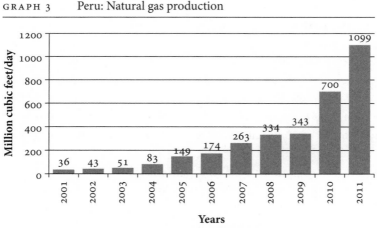

Source: Compiled by the author with data from Perupetro (2011).

had become largely unpopular among companies. By 2009 Peru hit a historical record with the signing of eighty-nine oil contracts (nineteen in the development phase and seventy exploration agreements), compared with a mere fourteen in 2004 (Ministry of Energy 2009). Investments in the oil industry are projected to reach US$9 billion in the period between 2010 and 2014 (Ministry of Economy 2013).

Despite the new oil exploration activity, Peru remains a minor crude producer compared with Colombia and Ecuador and still does not produce enough to meet domestic consumption, especially following the economic boom of the first decade of the twenty-first century. In 2008 and 2009 Peru produced 120,000 and 145,000 barrels per day, respectively, but consumption was higher, at 172,000 in 2008 and 188,000 in 2009 (BP 2009). Even in 2009, when domestic demand dropped as a consequence of the global economic recession, consumption was still higher than production of oil.

The expectation is that a free trade agreement Peru signed with China in 2009, plus exports of liquefied natural gas that started in 2010, will eventually produce a steady income to help offset increasing oil imports and stabilize the hydrocarbons trade balance. Peru's refining network has not yet been upgraded to process the country's mainly heavy crude blends, so imports of lighter oil are needed to mix the two and run them through domestic refineries. This situation would be reversed with the planned expansion and upgrading of the 62,000-barrels-per-day Talara refinery, which would allow for the processing of the domestically produced heavy crude without needing to import expensive lighter blends.

Peruvians were eagerly anticipating the planned start-up of production in 2013 of Block 67, located in the northern Amazon department of Loreto and thought to be the largest in Peru. The almost three hundred million barrels of heavy crude the Amazon block is estimated to hold are viewed as a potential solution to the country's oil deficit. However, opposition by the Indigenous population has been very strong and the future of Block 67, and adjacent Block 39, remains unclear.

OIL INVESTMENTS IN 2000 AND BEYOND

The region as a whole, with the exception of Ecuador and Venezuela, which adopted state-oriented policies, saw a boom in foreign direct investment (FDI)

GRAPH 4   Foreign direct investment flows to South America

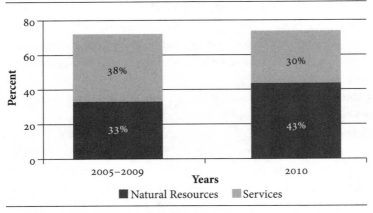

Source: Compiled by the author with data from ECLAC (2010a).

flows during the first decade of the twenty-first century. In 2010 FDI to Latin America surged by 56 percent over 2009 figures, and natural resources, including the oil and gas industries, were the sector of preference for investors. That year, general FDI to South America exceeded the annual average for the decade, reflecting the region's expanding role as an investment destination for transnational companies, oil corporations among them. Natural resources attracted 43 percent of the total FDI in 2010, followed by the service sector (United Nations 2010). As shown in graph 4, of the two main FDI recipient sectors, only natural resources saw an increase in 2010 from previous years.

The ups and downs of the oil industry in Latin America have been historically linked to the flow of private investment. Often, there is a direct link between the pace of increase or fall in production and reserves and the flow of FDI. With few exceptions, governments lack the human, technological, and financial capacity needed to sustain a dynamic oil and gas industry, and they need to resort to private investors.

As described earlier, during the first decade of the twenty-first century, private oil investments moved in opposite directions in Peru and Ecuador: while Lima saw an influx of oil investors, Quito experienced steep drops. The main reason for this trend was Peru's investor-friendly policies versus Ecuador's support of an increasing role of the state in its natural resource sector, particularly in oil and gas developments. Credible statistics for the hydrocarbons sector are elusive for Ecuador, but FDI flows for the whole natural resource sector are quite eloquent when compared with those of Peru. In 2009 Peru received US$443 million in FDI in natural resources, a notable increase from only US$65 million in 2001. By contrast, during the same period Ecuador experienced a huge decline of FDI in natural resources, from US$1.14 billion in 2001 to US$45 million in 2009 (CEPAL 2009). By comparison, in 2009 Colombia received US$5.8 billion in FDI for developing its natural resources, a significant increase from almost US$1.1 billion in 2001, mainly due to the country's decision to develop that sector with private investment.

In Peru, the creation of a state agency—Perupetro—in 1993 specifically for promoting oil investment in the hydrocarbons sector was the key to sustaining the success that followed. Private investment has been the main engine behind Peru's economic growth of the past two decades, and hydrocarbons have been the second most attractive investment sector after mining. To attract oil companies Peru introduced low royalty rates and flexible operating terms and throughout the 1990s started to incorporate a body of laws that guaranteed stable legal terms for investors.[9] The state adopted a smaller role in oil and gas exploration to allow for increased private participation, and by June 2010 it was considering lowering its stake in the state-owned oil company Petroperu by 20 percent. In 2005 the Peruvian Congress granted Petroperu complete autonomy to undertake exploration and development activities and to participate in the whole chain of the hydrocarbons process, in competition with other players.

By contrast, in Ecuador, following the 2010 reforms to the hydrocarbons law, private companies lost the right to keep a share of oil finds. They were required instead to hand over their oil production to the state. In exchange, they would receive a flat fee, which varied from contract to contract, for each barrel of produced oil. The departure of four major oil operators culminated in a string of events leading to a more assertive role for the state in the control of the oil industry during the first decade of the twenty-first century.

With a total of 250.2 million barrels of proven oil reserves, Latin America holds the second-largest global oil pool. That in itself would appear to be enough to attract investor interest to meet future global demand increase. However, most of the total reserve base is concentrated in Venezuela, which for the past two decades has been hostile to private investments. In 2011 Venezuela held 211.2 million barrels of oil reserves and 195.2 trillion cubic feet of natural gas: 15.3 percent of the world total oil reserves and 2.7 percent of its natural gas endowment (BP 2011). No wonder Venezuela has been the mecca for oil companies in South America, at least until the mid-1990s, when investment regulations were softer.

Had it not been that Venezuela's tightening of its investment rules at a time of high international oil prices made it feasible to develop economically risky Amazon areas, Peru and Colombia might have not experienced large investment flows. This is simply because Venezuela's large base of conventional and nonconventional oil and gas reserves and its low geological risk factors make that country a favorite among oil investors. The hydrocarbons reserve base in the three countries studied in this book is minimal. Table 3 shows the world share of crude and gas reserves among the main producing Latin American countries. Ecuador, Colombia, and Peru are highlighted.

In terms of production, in 2011 Latin America as a region contributed roughly 7.4 million barrels per day, or just 9.5 percent, of global oil output (BP 2011). Venezuela and Brazil together produced most of that, or almost 5 million barrels per day of oil. The other countries contributed minimal amounts to world output. Graph 5 shows Venezuela's role as South America's number

TABLE 3   Latin American oil and gas reserves (2011)

	Oil reserves (millions of barrels)	Share of world total (%)	Gas reserves (trillions of cubic feet)	Share of world total (%)
Venezuela	211.2	15.3	195.2	2.7
Brazil	15.1	0.9	16.0	0.2
Mexico	11.4	0.7	12.5	0.2
Ecuador	6.2	0.4	n/a	n/a
Argentina	2.5	0.2	12.0	0.2
Colombia	2.0	0.1	5.8	0.1
Peru	1.2	0.1	12.5	0.2
Bolivia	n/a	n/a	9.9	0.1
Trinidad and Tobago	0.8	0.1	14.2	0.2
Total	250.2	17.8	278.1	3.9

Source: Compiled by the author with data from BP (2011).

GRAPH 5   South America's main oil-producing countries (2011)

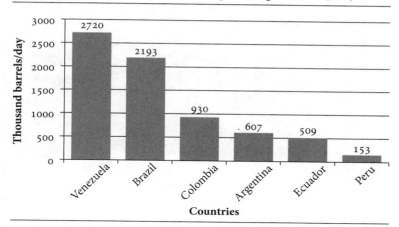

Source: Compiled by the author with data from BP (2011).

* Production figures for Colombia differ slightly between the official 786,000 barrels per day and the 801,000 barrels per day of BP's *Statistical Review*.

one oil producer, followed by Brazil, with Colombia as a distant third. Peru is a minor oil producer for the moment.

The oil scenario for the region will likely change dramatically once the bulk of Brazil's newly found hydrocarbons reserves, located in deep waters off the country's southern coast, are deemed commercial. Brazil plans to produce in excess of 4 million barrels per day by 2020, which would more than double the amount it produced in 2011. By then, Brazil will comfortably become Latin America's number one producer of oil, surpassing Mexico and Venezuela, which produced 3 million barrels per day and 2.72 million, respectively, in 2011 (EIA 2012b).

In December 2010 Brazil's state-controlled oil company Petrobras submitted a declaration of commerciality for two presalt fields, the Lula and Cernambi (formerly Tupi and Iracema), with an estimate of total recoverable reserves between the two of 8.3 billion barrels of oil equivalent (the combined values of crude oil and natural gas extraction). By some accounts, total deep-water crude reserves in all of the fields are estimated between 10 and 16 billion barrels of recoverable oil. Added to Brazil's proven crude reserves of 12.9 billion barrels, the deep and ultradeep finds would place the country second after Venezuela among largest Latin American hydrocarbons holders (IEA 2010, 114).

GRAPH 6   Natural gas producers (billions of cubic feet per day)

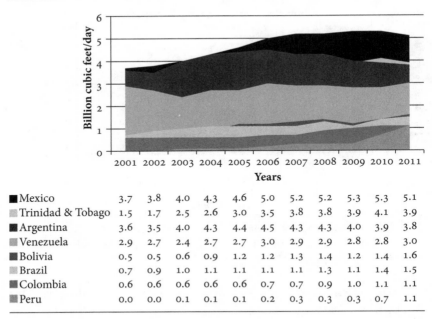

	2001	2002	2003	2004	2005	2006	2007	2008	2009	2010	2011
■ Mexico	3.7	3.8	4.0	4.3	4.6	5.0	5.2	5.2	5.3	5.3	5.1
▨ Trinidad & Tobago	1.5	1.7	2.5	2.6	3.0	3.5	3.8	3.8	3.9	4.1	3.9
■ Argentina	3.6	3.5	4.0	4.3	4.4	4.5	4.3	4.3	4.0	3.9	3.8
▨ Venezuela	2.9	2.7	2.4	2.7	2.7	3.0	2.9	2.9	2.8	2.8	3.0
■ Bolivia	0.5	0.5	0.6	0.9	1.2	1.2	1.3	1.4	1.2	1.4	1.6
▨ Brazil	0.7	0.9	1.0	1.1	1.1	1.1	1.1	1.3	1.1	1.4	1.5
■ Colombia	0.6	0.6	0.6	0.6	0.6	0.7	0.7	0.9	1.0	1.1	1.1
▨ Peru	0.0	0.0	0.1	0.1	0.1	0.2	0.3	0.3	0.3	0.7	1.1

Source: Compiled by the author with data from BP (2011).

The development of Brazil's presalt reserves will also change the natural gas landscape for the region. In 2011 Mexico in North America and Trinidad and Tobago in the Caribbean continued to be the main producers, at 5.1 trillion and 3.9 billion cubic feet per day, respectively (BP 2011). Colombia's natural gas production has been increasing steadily since 2001: from 600 million to 1.1 billion cubic feet per day in 2010, when it was still producing more than Peru. But Peru caught up in 2011 with a matching of 1.1 billion cubic feet per day output, reflecting the country's impressive performance since the startup of production in 2003 from its massive Camisea gas reserves. Ecuador's natural gas production is marginal, and for that reason it is not included in this analysis. Graph 6 shows Latin America's main natural gas-producing countries.

Latin America is expected to contribute a significant share of world oil supply to meet demands projected for the near future. For that to happen, the region will need major investments to modernize its decaying infrastructure. International Energy Agency (2010, 94) calculations estimate that a cumulative global investment of US$8.1 billion will be needed in energy supply infrastructure between 2010 and 2035 to meet world oil and gas supply projections. Most of the oil supply infrastructure investments will be in non-OECD countries, with Latin America taking the first place among them.

SUMMARY

Investor interest in oil and gas in South America has grown tremendously in the past two decades, and the region is starting to be seen as a potential major source of global oil supplies for the near future. High international oil prices and sound investment policies in some countries have contributed to the region's hydrocarbons boom. In coming decades South America will continue to be among the regions of choice for oil investors, due to strong global demand and high oil prices, which are both projected to remain robust. This is in spite of the fact that the region holds only 15 percent of total world oil reserves, compared with 57 percent in the Middle East. Political turmoil and uncertainty in the Middle East has resulted in dwindling investor interest that will likely contribute to a refocusing on other regions with potential, such as Latin America.

One of the new areas of interest is the western Amazon, where oil and gas reserves have until recently remained largely untapped, due to inaccessibility and environmental and social risks. High international oil prices and increasingly scant conventional oil pools around the world suddenly put this previously forgotten and remote part of the globe on the radar screen of oil companies. While an attractive oil investment area under current market conditions, the western Amazon retains the social and environmental characteristics that had kept investor interest at arm's length for many years: the presence and opposition of historically marginalized vulnerable groups, mainly Indigenous populations, and a unique biological diversity, both of which pose an enormous risk for oil development. The clash between the development impulse and the conservationist forces is at the heart of the unparalleled proliferation of oil-related conflicts that have emerged in the region. Unless rapidly and effectively resolved, these conflicts threaten the long-term sustainability of economic growth in Latin America.

CHAPTER 2

Indigenous Peoples and Natural Resource Development

THE HYDROCARBONS-RELATED conflicts in the Andean countries analyzed in this book involve mainly Indigenous populations. This minority group is the poorest and most marginalized in Peru and Ecuador, and to a lesser extent in Colombia, where Afro-Colombians are the largest, most vulnerable group. Indigenous Peoples remain largely underrepresented in the domestic political and institutional life of all three countries.

This situation persists despite a growing movement for the recognition of the rights of Indigenous Peoples that made major gains in the past two decades, both domestically and internationally. Indigenous demands go beyond economic grievances and include a right to proper institutional and political participation and, most important, to land ownership. They also demand recognition of their right to speak different languages and to engage in specific cultural practices, such as the use of plants for medicinal cures or adherence to customary law. Their demands have been highlighted with the arrival of oil and gas projects, which they view as an invasion of their territory bringing little in the way of improvements to their living standards. Indigenous grievances underlie most oil and gas conflicts in the region.

HOW FAR DOES INDIGENOUS RECOGNITION GO?

The search for recognition by the Indigenous population of Latin America is not new and can be traced back to the colonial period, with natural resources always playing a fundamental role. In the colonial days Indians were removed from their lands and forced to become manual laborers (Grey Postero 2007, 27–36). In Bolivia, Aymara and Kichwa Indians became *pongo* laborers, serving the hacienda owners or miners in the departments of Potosí, Oruro, and La Paz. At the time of the Spanish colonization, Potosí became the main supplier of silver to the Spanish Crown from a mountain that had such huge accumulations of silver ore that it was named Cerro Rico (rich mountain). The lavishness prompted by the exuberant mineral wealth of the Spanish colonies at the time of the colonization was famously described in a novel by Uruguayan author Eduardo Galeano:

> The church altars and the wings of cherubim in processions for the Corpus Christi celebration in 1658, were made of silver: the streets from the cathedral to the church of Recoletos were completely resurfaced with silver bars. In Potosí, silver built temples and palaces, monasteries and gambling dens; it prompted tragedies and fiestas, led to the spilling of blood and wine, fired avarice, and unleashed extravagance and adventure. (Galeano 1997, 20)

The luxuries of colonial Spain that were built on the newly discovered treasures greatly contrasted with the inhuman living conditions of Indigenous populations in the Americas. Not only were they forced to work as quasi slaves in plantations, mines, and public and religious construction undertaken by the Spanish, but their lands were seized and given to Spanish noblemen and colonists. Repression of any opposition was severe.

The Indigenous population staged several revolts against the treatment they received from the Spanish colonizers. Particularly noteworthy was the 1780 Indigenous uprising in Peru led by Tupac Amaru II, born José Miguel Condorcanqui. An inhabitant of Cuzco, and of royal Inca descent, he worked for the Spanish Crown and was educated by the Jesuits. He tried to improve the conditions of Indigenous workers, but when he met with serious resistance from his masters, he adopted his great-grandfather's name, Tupac Amaru, and staged an all-out rebellion. The struggle was quashed by the colonial power and all the Indigenous leaders were savagely executed. Subsequent efforts by the church, and in particular the Jesuits, as illustrated in the 1986 award-winning film *The Mission*, largely failed to improve the overall conditions of the Indigenous population until much later, after independence.

Following the assimilation policies at the end of the 1880s came another period of slave-like conditions for the Indians, this time brought about by the profitable rubber industry in the jungle. The inhuman working conditions in Peru were much publicized at the time and even turned into a diplomatic scandal in 1911, when following denunciations by then British consul Roger Casement, the British Parliament opened an investigation on the role played by British Peruvian Amazon Company in the torture and slavery of Indigenous workers (Vélez Araujo 2008). The atrocities of the time in the Peruvian Ama-

zon were vividly depicted by Peruvian writer and Nobel Prize winner Mario
Vargas Llosa:

> Every two weeks the harvesters returned to the station to bring in the rubber.
> This was weighted on the dishonest scales. If after three months they had not
> fulfilled thirty kilos, they received punishments that ranged from floggings
> to the pillory, cutting off ears and noses, or in extreme cases, the torture and
> killing of the wife, children, and the harvester himself. The corpses were not
> buried but dragged into the forest to be eaten by the animals. . . .
>
> . . . Dyall confessed to Roger and the commission that one day at the
> Matanzas station, Normand ordered him to kill five Andoques as punish-
> ment for not having met their rubber quotas. Dyall shot the first two, but the
> manager ordered that for the next two he should first crush their testicles
> with a stone for grinding yucca and then finish them off by garroting them.
> He had him strangle the last one with his bare hands. During the entire op-
> eration Normand sat on a tree trunk, smoking and watching, with no change
> in the indolent expression on his reddish face. (Vargas Llosa 2010, 180–82)

Organized efforts by Indigenous Peoples to try to undo the ethnic segregation
or forced assimilation imposed in the postcolonial period started in the 1940s,
with the first Indigenous organizations created in Ecuador. In some ways oil
trailed rubber as a source of conflict and major injustices.

The land reforms that spread throughout the continent in the 1960s supported important programs of land redistribution among peasants (*campesinos* in Spanish). This created an incentive for Indigenous Peoples to register as
peasants, a new social class that gained access to state-run social services and
was devoid of any ethnic characterization (Yashar 1999).The underlying goal of
the reforms was to dilute the Indigenous identity and to build a homogeneous
concept for citizenship that would prevail in each country. Governments were
trying to create one citizenship, devoid of ethnic or cultural particularities, by
assimilating Indians into the mainstream population. There was a shared belief
among the ruling classes at the time that to be able to achieve modernization,
countries needed to sustain a homogeneous culture, one that would absorb the
various ethnic and cultural identities, along with their histories, languages, customs, and beliefs (Marc 2010, 14–16). This strong push for the assimilation of
Indigenous populations through a policy of land reform took place to various
degrees in most Latin American countries.

But while governments created a new homogeneous class of small farmers, many Indigenous Peoples cultivated their Indian identity inwardly (Lucero 2008, 139–68). This was especially true in remote areas like the Amazon, where the lack of a strong government presence created the conditions for the survival of Indigenous political identities and institutions that have prevailed since the colonial period. Indigenous populations also created new organizations to promote their identities, which were often at odds with the policies of assimilation of central governments (Yashar 1999). The power of this connection to an Indigenous ethnic identity, particularly in the remote Amazon jungle, survived the assimilation policies of the time and became instrumental in the development of the organized social Indigenous movement that took shape twenty years later.

The economic policies of the 1980s were matched politically by the beginning of democratization in Latin America, after decades of military regimes that had restricted civil liberties and freedom of expression. This period saw a burst of Indigenous activism throughout the region, in part as a consequence of domestic reforms that encouraged popular participation, but largely in response to increasingly active support by the international community for the recognition of the rights of Indigenous Peoples. The fall of the Berlin wall in 1989 and the disappearance of ideological competition between the capitalist and communist blocs have been widely identified as a turning point for social movements around the world that left behind the class-based focus characteristic of the Cold War era. In Latin America, Indigenous movements, particularly in the Andean countries, started to establish international alliances to fight for regional recognition.

The strengthening and internationalization of the Indigenous movement was supported by constitutional reforms at home for the incorporation of the rights and the acceptance of a specific identity for this minority group. Also key in spreading the Indigenous cause was the naissance of an international body of law for the recognition of Indigenous rights. International jurisprudence continues to have a tremendous influence even today, gradually and steadily advancing the legal recognition of Indigenous rights. Some countries witnessed in Indigenous movements the emergence of new social and political actors that started to challenge traditional political structures and were instrumental in reshaping states' development and political agendas (Bello 2008, 48–65). By putting communal land claims at the heart of the discussion, Indigenous groups were also asserting their historical claim for a cultural recognition that emphasizes the collective over the individual. Land ownership is one of the most controversial issues surrounding oil- and gas-related conflicts.

In the 1990s Indigenous movements made major strides in expanding their agenda, both at home and internationally, for achieving political participation and improved living conditions. It was to a large extent growing Indigenous activism that led to increasing recognition and acceptance of Indigenous groups in Peru, Ecuador, and Colombia. The three countries introduced changes to their constitutions, laws, and institutions to support better inclusion of these minority groups.

In Ecuador the 1998 Constitution incorporated the concept of multiculturalism, largely as a result of increasing political activism by the Confederación de Nacionalidades Indígenas del Ecuador. Created in 1986, this Indigenous organization—Ecuador's largest—had become politically active by 1996 by forming an alliance with non-Indigenous groups and by creating the Pachakutik Pluricultural Movement. The 1998 Constitution gave specific rights to Indigenous Peoples for preserving their culture and their political organizations. An additional constitutional reform in 2008 stated that while natural resources belong to the state, Indigenous Peoples should be consulted when resource development directly affects them.

In Peru the 1979 Law of Communities recognized Indigenous rights to lands that were demarcated, and as a result land titles were granted to Indigenous groups for the first time. The law contributed to the organization of Indigenous populations in the Amazon into communities. Many authors criticized it for isolating Indigenous Peoples and for arbitrarily grouping them in different territories. But the legislation has been commended by some scholars as the most advanced recognition of Indigenous rights in Latin America at the time (Gray 2003, 74–89).

In Colombia the Constitutional Court, since its creation in 1991, produced various legal resolutions in favor of Indigenous Peoples that have been praised as unique in the world.[1] The creation of the Constitutional Court itself was quite exceptional in the region and constituted an important step for the protection of Indigenous rights. The Constitutional Court is a tribunal specifically geared toward protecting and guaranteeing the rights of citizens. The 1991 Constitution also introduced the judicial concept of *tutela* (writ of protection), which is aimed at protecting the fundamental constitutional rights of citizens and considered to be the backbone behind the incorporation of Indigenous rights in

Colombia. Furthermore, the 1991 Constitution instituted two congressional seats for Indigenous representatives and stipulated that a percentage of federal funds should be allocated to municipal budgets and to Indigenous communities (Wirpsa and Dunning 2004).

These important domestic steps were parallel to the rapid development of recognition of Indigenous Peoples and minority rights worldwide. International recognition of Indigenous Peoples' rights goes back to 1957, with the adoption of the International Labor Organization (ILO) Convention 107, which was the first international attempt at addressing Indigenous concerns. But the convention was controversial because it was based on the theory of integration and assimilation prevalent at the time, while placing little value on the protection of the unique characteristics of Indigenous cultures and cultural rights (Anaya 2005, 78–96; Wiessner 1999, 57).

By 1989 much of the controversy was resolved with the signing of the new ILO Convention 169: Concerning Indigenous and Tribal Peoples in Independent Countries. The new binding convention went far beyond the previous one in promoting the integrity of Indigenous culture, as well as the sovereignty of Indigenous communities over their lands and resources (Anaya 2005, 96–100). In essence, it gave Indigenous communities the right to live according to their own distinctive customs, recommending that states respect their objectives in all decisions concerning them. The new convention was a major step toward the adoption by governments of concrete standards for treating Indigenous Peoples, although its wording in the form of *recommendations* rather than *norms* was much criticized (99). The language used by the convention reflects the reluctance of many states to recognize the right of Indigenous self-determination— illustrated by the convention's refusal to use the word *peoples* because of the association of this term with the right to form an independent state (100–102). Convention 169 is the main international legal instrument cited in disputes over oil and gas that involve Indigenous Peoples.

In 2004 the United Nations went further in highlighting the importance of the Indigenous issue when the General Assembly proclaimed 2005–14 as the second consecutive International Decade of the World's Indigenous People. The period from 1995 to 2004 was characterized by an upsurge of Indigenous mobilization, demanding greater political participation and better living conditions. Indigenous populations did indeed experience considerable gains in terms of political representation and access to positions of power at that time. Their protests forced multicultural development into the mainstream of politics (Lucero 2008, 139–68). However, it was clear that the international debate on cultural rights did not significantly serve to improve the living conditions of Indigenous Peoples. In fact, in some cases their living standards even deteriorated, which prompted the United Nations to highlight the issue for a second decade.

The objective of the second decade was to strengthen international cooperation to solve problems faced by Indigenous Peoples in areas such as culture, education, health, human rights, the environment, and social and economic development. As part of these developments, the United Nations adopted the Universal Declaration on the Rights of Indigenous Peoples.[2] The adoption of the declaration was not easy; it was the result of more than twenty years of negotiation. The declaration emphasizes in its introduction the importance of territorial control for Indigenous Peoples' culture:

> Control by indigenous peoples over developments affecting them and their lands, territories and resources will enable them to maintain and strengthen their institutions, cultures and traditions, and to promote their development in accordance with their aspirations and needs. (United Nations 2007, 2)

The declaration is seen as a vital step in proclaiming the right to self-determination for Indigenous Peoples, as stated in article 3. This means, among other matters, that Indigenous groups should have some level of freedom to adopt their own internal policies and to make use of their natural resource endowments. On the latter, however, they must abide by international economic cooperation obligations, based on international law and the principle of mutual benefit (García Hierro and Surrallés 2009, 18–29). The nonbinding declaration went beyond Convention 169 by incorporating the controversial concept of self-determination with regard to Indigenous communities, the land they live on, and the natural resources that surround them. The introduction to the declaration includes the words, "Bearing in mind that nothing in this Declaration may be used to deny any peoples their right to self-determination, exercised in conformity with international law" (Anaya 2005, 114–18, 3).

Over the years discussions about these international documents have forged the basis of a quasi-universal consensus about the rights of Indigenous Peoples, based on general human rights principles in widely ratified treaties. Some scholars argue these developments can be understood as giving rise to a body of customary law on Indigenous rights, when particular customs within a community become the norm and are generally accepted as such (Anaya 2009, 13–61). The United Nations incorporated several mechanisms for approaching Indigenous questions, including the Permanent Forum on Indigenous Issues, a special rapporteur on Human Rights and Fundamental Liberties of Indigenous Peoples, and an Inter-Agency Support Group on Indigenous Issues. The Permanent Forum is especially noteworthy because it constitutes the first time that Indigenous populations have direct access to the United Nations. The sixteen members of the forum are independent experts acting on their behalf, with eight chosen by the Indigenous Peoples themselves and the remaining eight selected by governments.

These moves in favor of Indigenous Peoples have been supported by a general acceptance that integration of minority groups requires some recognition of specific cultural rights. This recognition has called into question previous assumptions about the importance of assimilation to support a modern state. One of the most influential theorists on cultural rights, Will Kymlicka, writes,

> I believe it is legitimate, and indeed unavoidable, to supplement traditional human rights with minority rights. A comprehensive theory of justice in a multicultural state will include both universal rights, assigned to individuals regardless of group membership, and certain group-differentiated rights or "special status" for minority culture. (1995, 6)

In 1989 the General Assembly of the Organization of American States (OAS) requested that the Inter-American Commission on Human Rights prepare a legal instrument on the rights of Indigenous Peoples. The declaration was meant to be approved by the General Assembly as a symbol of the willingness of American governments to recognize Indigenous rights. But twenty years and several drafts later, the OAS has yet to come up with a document on Indigenous Peoples' rights that reflects their demands. The original declaration, presented by the commission in 1997, lacked Indigenous Peoples' input and reflected the methodology then used: debates behind closed doors by OAS working groups for drafting the document. Indigenous Peoples were not officially recognized as participants in the OAS working groups together with member states until 2003. By contrast, the final revision of the declaration currently under consideration is more inclusive and reflects discussions among member state delegations, NGOs, and Indigenous representatives (Permanent Council 2010).

It soon became obvious that such an advanced body of international laws, with far-reaching cultural and political minority rights, would be difficult to monitor and especially to impose on countries. For that reason, much emphasis was placed on the establishment of a balanced dialogue between Indigenous populations and the rest of society, including the government. The underlying goal of Convention 169 is to institute an intercultural instrument in the hope that it will eventually bring parties closer to achieving common ground.

Even more significant for the impact on conflicts about investment in hydrocarbons is the adoption by large multilateral organizations of safeguards related to Indigenous populations. The World Bank and its private sector branch, the International Finance Corporation, have compiled policies on Indigenous populations that redirected the way these multilateral institutions invest in areas populated by Indigenous communities. The World Bank policy on Indigenous Peoples underscores the need for borrowers and bank staff to identify Indigenous Peoples and to consult with them and ensure their participation in and benefit from operations funded by the bank (World Bank 2005). The Inter-American Development Bank promotes development policies that respect the identity of Indigenous Peoples. In the case of natural resources, it specifically supports policies that include consultation with Indigenous Peoples, their participation in resource management, and the sharing of benefits resulting from projects developed on their lands (IADB 2006).

But these safeguards have become controversial, because Indigenous representative organizations have contested the extent of the consultation process. They demand the inclusion of the concept of "free, prior and informed consent," as stated by the UN Declaration on the Rights of Indigenous Peoples (2007), that would give them the right to veto a World Bank project. The bank policies accept this concept in general terms, but they specifically refrain from giving Indigenous Peoples veto power. The World Bank Operational Policy on Indigenous Peoples reads,

> *Consultation and Participation.* Where the project affects Indigenous Peoples, the borrower engages in free, prior, and informed consultation with them. (Article 10)
>
> The Bank reviews the process and the outcome of the consultation carried out by the borrower to satisfy itself that the affected Indigenous Peoples' communities have provided their broad support to the project. The Bank pays particular attention to the social assessment and to the record and out-

come of the free, prior, and informed consultation with the affected Indigenous Peoples' communities as a basis for ascertaining whether there is such support. The Bank does not proceed further with project processing if it is unable to ascertain that such support exists. (Article 11)

Free, prior, and informed consultation with the affected Indigenous Peoples' communities refers to a culturally appropriate and collective decision-making process. It does not constitute a veto right for individuals or groups. (Note 4)

Recently there has been increasing realization that the rapid development of international norms for supporting minority and Indigenous Peoples' rights has created a critical gap between the reality in the field and the ambitious safeguards introduced from outside. There is also a general sense that the debate on minority rights has gone too far. Some European countries and newly emerging markets, such as China and India, have expressed concern about the effect that increased minority rights could have on the national cohesion of their societies.

LIMITATIONS TO ECONOMIC AND POLITICAL INCLUSION

Latin America is a good example of the fact that the numerous national and international norms to protect the rights of Indigenous Peoples have a limited impact on improving the livelihood of this marginalized sector of society. The region maintains deep inequities, even after some progress over the past decade, particularly in relation to poverty reduction. Indigenous populations in the three countries under study are among the most affected by these inequalities and form a large part of the poor and extremely poor. It is these populations that are directly affected by oil and natural gas projects.

Persistent social and economic inequality is probably the most pervasive unresolved social problem in Latin America, overshadowing growth-related progress. In 2010, a full 32.1 percent of Latin Americans—or 180 million—still lived in poverty, and 12.9 percent—equivalent to 72 million—in extreme poverty. As striking as they may look, these figures still represent a strong improvement from 1990, when 48.3 percent of Latin Americans were beneath the poverty level (United Nations 2010, 17–20). Income inequalities were reduced in the past decade, due to the expansion of basic education that helped to close the income gap between skilled and low-skilled workers and to increased government transfers to the poor. The Gini Coefficient for the region declined by an average 1.1 percent per year (López-Calva and Lustig 2010, 18).[3]

But social disparities are still very large and most evident in four basic areas. First, disparities in levels of income have historically been extremely high: household surveys between 1989 and 2001 show that the richest 10 percent of the population receives between 40 percent and 47 percent of total income (De Ferranti et al. 2004, 37–76). Second, access to basic services such as education, health care, and drinking water is still far from universal. Despite much progress since the 1990s, disparities in sanitation coverage, particularly between rural and urban areas, remain high. The extent of sanitation coverage in rural Latin America was on average below 50 percent in 2010 (UNICEF–World Health Organization 2012, 19). Access to drinking water among the rural population of western Latin America was as low as only 50 percent that year, compared to almost 100 percent among the urban population (13). In Peru, about three out of ten households within the lowest quintile in the society have access to drinking water, compared to nine out of ten in the uppermost quintile (Gasparini et al. 2009).

The third disparity, related to land distribution and ownership, is probably the most controversial as far as oil and gas development is concerned. Inequitable land ownership has been a typical feature of Latin American countries, which have a history of incomplete or inefficient land reforms throughout the twentieth century. Land reforms have mostly been focused on achieving a more equitable distribution in the size of plots per farmer but not so much on how the newly distributed plots would be developed. In Peru, for example, the redistribution of land from landowners to farmworkers that took place in the 1950s and 1960s was not accompanied by programs to promote an efficient development of the newly acquired areas. This could be one of the reasons for today's high poverty levels among many of the peasant owners of those redistributed lands (De Janvry and Sadoulet 2002).

Throughout Latin America, land ownership rights are unclear or nonexistent, which creates disputes when trying to define borders for the development of natural resource projects. Ambiguous property rights in turn may reduce investment incentives for developing the land and may affect the ability to use it as collateral for credit. Landholding elites that built political influence through the ownership of huge territories have largely disappeared. But there is still a minority of poor people in the region whose access to land has been historically contested but whose identity is paradoxically directly connected to the territory they live in. These are Indigenous communities, especially in the Amazon region, for whom their land is not only a source of livelihood but also a symbol of identity passed on through generations.

Last, Latin American countries also show large inequities in relation to the number of people who have political decision-making power and also with regard to those who benefit from the rule of law. Historically, Latin American countries have shown an entrenched pattern of clientelism and corruption, usually determined by the extent of influence individuals or groups can exert on the authorities to advance their own interests. Wealthy individuals or companies generally have more access to the state than those in lower levels of the society. In the 2010 Transparency International Corruption Perceptions Index, Peru and Colombia both ranked 78 of a total of 178 countries (50). That was three levels down from the 2009 ranking, when both countries occupied the 75th place of a total of 180 (45–49). Ecuador was by far the worst of the three, as it ranked 146 in 2009, although it saw an improvement the following year, when it occupied the 127th place. This is an index based on perceptions rather than on actual deeds; however, its results reflect that Latin Americans have little confidence that they have fair and effective governmental institutions.

In highly unequal societies like those of Latin America, relatively new democratic institutions are prone to manipulation by the educated elites or other influential groups that use them for their own particular benefits (Perry 2008, 50). Such manipulation has serious impacts on equality because economically disadvantaged groups lack the tools for accessing the authorities through parallel channels. In Latin America the exchange of favors for benefits is still common practice. Politicians try to get popular support by providing material goods to meet immediate needs rather than by implementing public policies that will provide these goods on a sustainable, long-term basis. On the other end, clientelistic relationships undermine the organization of voters and their demands for the development of well-functioning public services.

In Latin America inequality has a strong ethnic component, and Indigenous populations in general, and Afro-Colombians in Colombia in particular—constituting roughly 11 percent of the total population, or 4.4 million—are especially affected (DANE 2005). Poverty rates decreased in most countries across the region throughout the 1990s; however, the situation changed little for Indigenous People during that time. Indigenous Peoples work mainly in agriculture

GRAPH 7   Ecuador: Percentage of poor according to ethnicity

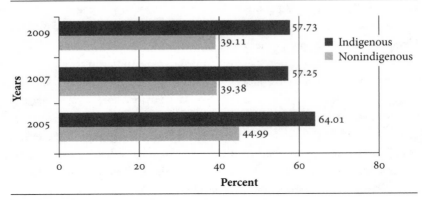

Source: Compiled by the author with data from ECLAC (2010d).

as self-employed workers, and their salaries tend to be significantly lower than those of their non-Indigenous counterparts. Ethnicity may not only account for lower income or wealth but can also be related to lower education levels and fewer employment opportunities in most Latin American countries (Atal, Nopo, and Winder 2009).

Graph 7 compares poverty levels between Indigenous and non-Indigenous groups in Ecuador over a five-year period (2005 to 2009). In 2005 an astonishing 64 percent of the Indigenous population in Ecuador was poor, compared with 45 percent of non-Indigenous. While overall poverty levels improved in 2009, the gap between Indigenous and non-Indigenous persisted, 58 percent versus almost 40 percent, respectively (ECLAC 2010c).

Since 1985 Ecuador incorporated bilingual education for Indigenous children as part of the country's official curriculum; however, Indigenous children have still to gain access to quality schooling. This mirrors overall statistics for the region, where Indigenous Peoples have on average less access to formal education—only 4.3 years of schooling, compared with 6.9 years for non-Indigenous Peoples (Larrea and Montenegro Torres 2006). In addition, 43 percent of Indigenous children who go to school also work, which makes it difficult for them to stay in school on a regular basis, and they often suffer from malnutrition, which has been linked to poor education outcomes. According to the 2001 national census, only 58 percent of Indigenous children between the ages of five and eighteen went to school and did not work, compared with 73 percent among non-Indigenous groups. Infant mortality rates among Indigenous children are more than double—10.5 percent versus 5.1 percent—those of the non-Indigenous population in the 2001 census data (INEC 2001).

Peru shows the most improvement in terms of poverty reduction among Indigenous communities in the past decade, but the differences with non-Indigenous groups is still striking. Between 25 percent and 48 percent of Peruvian households can be considered Indigenous, measured by the number of members that speak an Indigenous language (Trivelli 2006). Graph 8 shows comparative poverty levels for Indigenous and non-Indigenous groups for 2001, 2008, and 2009. Poverty among Indigenous groups went down to 55 percent in 2009 from an astonishing 82 percent in 2001. But during the same years, the number of poor among the non-Indigenous population was also reduced: 29 percent in 2009 and 50 percent in 2001.

Generally speaking, some 66 percent of Peruvian non-Indigenous households have access to drinking water and 53 percent to sewage facilities, while among Indigenous groups those figures drop to 53 percent and 30 percent, respectively (Trivelli 2006).

By 2011 Colombia did not have ethnically differentiated official data on poverty. The official data measured poverty levels overall but not by ethnic groups. The country managed to reduce overall poverty from 54 percent of the total population in 2002 to 46 percent in 2008, and indigence figures also decreased during that period, from 20 percent to 18 percent. But poverty indicators remain relatively high for a country that has averaged 5 percent annual Gross

GRAPH 8   Peru: Percentage of poor according to ethnicity

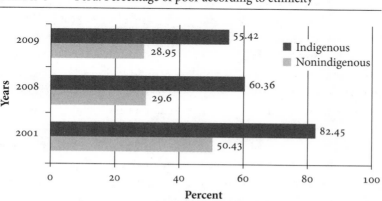

Source: Compiled by the author with data from ECLAC (2010d).

Domestic Product growth rates in recent years, in part thanks to oil and gas revenues. In 2008 Colombia had the third highest incidence of poverty and indigence in South America, after Bolivia and Paraguay (ECLAC 2010c, 18).

Nonofficial studies show higher percentages of illiteracy for Indigenous groups and Afro-Colombians—14.9 percent and 15.2 percent, respectively— versus 8.1 percent for nonethnic groups, according to data for 2003 (Urrea Giraldo and Viafara López 2007, 60–66). Health indicators are especially negative for Afro-Colombians living in rural areas, of whom only 34 percent have access to health care, compared with more than 55 percent for Indigenous and nonethnic groups (Bernal and Cardenas 2005).

Child labor is the norm for 75 percent of Indigenous children living in rural areas and 60 percent of Afro-Colombians living in urban centers (Urrea Giraldo and Viafara López 2007, 71–72). By some accounts, Indigenous and Afro-Colombian groups constitute as much as 40 percent of the total population, displaced as a consequence of the country's armed conflict (80). The loss of land assets has had a direct effect on the real poverty of these groups.

FROM SPARKS TO EXPLOSIONS

By 2008 at least thirty-five oil companies were developing 180 oil and gas blocks in the western Amazon, some of which overlapped with biodiversity-rich areas and regions inhabited by Indigenous groups, some living in voluntary isolation (Finer et al. 2008). The increased presence of oil and gas developments in areas inhabited by Indigenous populations that remain economically underprivileged and marginalized and whose land tenure status is unclear at best has proved to be an inevitable recipe for conflict. Moreover, many of these groups feel that the arrival of hydrocarbons development in the territories where they live challenges the survival of their culture and traditions and leaves them with little economic benefit in exchange. The conflicts around hydrocarbons also have become a means for Indigenous organizations to assert their broader claims for a strong role in the political life of the nation and for the recognition of their cultural distinctiveness.

Peru is a particularly graphic example of the struggling forces that normally shape the oil scenario in remote areas inhabited by poor Indigenous populations. Since the beginning of the twenty-first century, successive governments have focused their efforts on quickly developing the country's oil and natural gas reserves to make Peru self-sufficient in oil production and an exporter of

GRAPH 9   Peru: Oil contracts versus conflicts

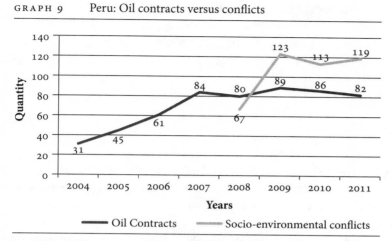

Source: Compiled by the author with data from the Ministry of Energy and Mines of Peru (2009) and the Office of the Ombudsman of Peru (2012).

natural gas. With economic growth, demand for hydrocarbons has increased. But oil imports at a time of high international oil prices became a source of major financial stress that governments were determined to minimize through the development of new and increased oil and gas reserves. The number of oil contracts in Peru rose threefold, from just thirty-one in 2004 to eighty-nine in 2009. But as oil licenses multiplied, so did the number of socioenvironmental conflicts, including those related specifically to oil and gas projects. Graph 9 illustrates the increasing trend in the number of oil contracts in Peru between 2004 and 2011 (see oil contracts line). In 2008 socioenvironmental conflicts in general, which include oil and gas disputes, shot up and reached a peak of 123 in 2009.

The new oil and gas projects particularly affected Indigenous areas: the northern Amazon, home to the Jivaroan and Urarina groups; the central jungle, which includes the territories of the Ashaninka, Nomatsiguenga, and Yanesha peoples; and the southern jungle department of Madre de Dios, home to the Camisea natural gas development and to the Harakmbut, Machiguenga, and Yine peoples.

Of the 89 hydrocarbons concessions active in 2009, the highest number in the history of the country, 70 were exploration contracts, up from 14 in 2004 (Ministry of Energy 2009). The Amazon housed 63 contracts, of which 46 overlapped with officially recognized Indigenous lands. A total of 17 developments coincided with proposed or already designated territorial areas for Indigenous Peoples living in voluntary isolation, who hold no formal land title yet. Also, 29 of the concessions overlapped with natural reserves that are protected or internationally recognized for their wealth in biodiversity (Orta-Martinez and Finer 2010).

SUMMARY

Local conflicts have developed parallel to—and in some cases as a consequence of—rapid growth in investment in oil and gas in the region. The quest for increased recognition of Indigenous People's rights and their struggle for improving their living conditions came together in opposition to oil projects, especially in the western Amazon basin. Underlying that trend were deeply rooted inequalities that have historically characterized Latin American societies and that particularly affect Indigenous populations.

The proliferation of oil and gas licenses coincided with an increasingly active, and sometimes politicized, Indigenous movement that is not shy about putting its demands forward, particularly in defense of its rights to property in the Amazon. Supporting that Indigenous activism is a large international and domestic body of laws created to safeguard Indigenous rights. But for Indigenous Peoples, none of those gains was enough when it came to sheltering their territories from oil and gas developments. The right to own land has historically been one of the main sources of conflict and still remains largely unresolved. Also contributing to the disputes around oil and gas is an imperfect legal system and governance flaws at the national and subnational levels that prevent an equitable distribution of the new hydrocarbons revenues.

CHAPTER 3

Structural Causes of Local Conflicts

IMPERFECT GOVERNANCE SYSTEMS that preclude participatory mechanisms or prevent revenues from being fairly distributed are the source of many oil-related local conflicts. Also contributing to these disputes are malfunctioning legal systems or a weak presence of the state in hydrocarbons producing areas. These flaws are structural in nature because they are usually embedded in the core of the democratic machinery and are difficult to modify.

Latin American countries have gone a long way in adopting and consolidating democratic government systems. Since the end of the 1980s, democracies, defined in 1942 by the minimalist economist Joseph Schumpeter as based on the transfer of power through free, fair, and regular elections, have been the rule rather than the exception (1962). The region has been part of a global trend that Samuel Huntington (1992, 23) called "the third wave of democracy" to describe the spread of democratic governments throughout the world in the 1970s and 1990s. With the arrival of democracy came the possibility to freely express discontent or different political views. With a few exceptions, Latin Americans can generally express their points of view today without fear of state repression or persecution of the kind the region suffered during past decades of military governments.

However, structural flaws still prevail and constitute a major obstacle to good governance. Institutions in Latin America have yet to strengthen the democratic system to prevent the use of violence as a way of expressing grievances. Building stronger democracies calls for the consolidation of political movements throughout the region, the development of popular trust in that process, and the strengthening of constitutional norms (Linz and Stepan 1996, 3–66). Furthermore, the region has yet to acquire systems of effective government accountability and, in particular, what has been defined as horizontal accountability: mechanisms by which one government entity holds another accountable (O'Donnell 1998).

Structural flaws have usually been in place for extended periods of time and are firmly established in the overall system of governance in Latin American democracies. Because a large percentage of the population has learned to live with them, and in some cases to benefit from them, very often there is perverse interest in keeping the flaws unchanged rather than solving them. Structural flaws end up configuring an atmosphere of institutional, legal, political, and social mismanagement that eventually creates a climate of conflict, challenging the very essence of democratic values.

Research has shown that democracies put up fewer barriers to participation than other, more repressive, government systems, and in that context minorities often tend to resort to protests, and not rebellion, to express discontent (Gurr 2000b). When people can express disapproval of the system through peaceful channels provided by the democratic institutions—such as voting, social protests, strikes, marches, or public dialogue—or when the institutional framework allows for their expression of discontent, they will be normally less inclined to resort to violence as a mechanism of last resort to communicate their problems. But in the presence of structural flaws that set limitations to open participation or to the promotion of public self-expression and accountability of the authorities, violence is bound to occur at some point. Probably the most obvious recent example of the extremes this process may reach is the succession of uprisings that swept the Middle East throughout 2011 (*Economist* 2011).

In the case of conflicts in Latin American oil- and gas-producing countries, the strong presence of a minority Indigenous population adds another dimension to an already complex scenario. The global trend toward democratization experienced in the 1990s contributed to improving the status of minority groups around the world and therefore to reducing tensions between them and the rest of the population (Gurr 2000a). A participatory democracy usually provides early warnings of potential tensions that, if properly and promptly addressed, may serve to prevent later explosions. But even when populations do have access to peaceful mechanisms for solving differences, violence can still erupt, particularly when governance weaknesses prevent democratic channels from responding to the needs of the population. When government institutions at local or national levels fail to operate in a transparent way or are seen as not representing the interests of the population, there is high potential for violent conflicts. Violence in this case becomes a tool for expressing dissatisfaction and a means for forcing government institutions to fulfill their obligations.

The following pages address some of the institutional and legal flaws that directly or indirectly contribute to the development of local conflicts in the presence of oil or gas reserves. Particular attention is given to the interplay between structural flaws, Indigenous groups, and the increasing trend to develop oil and gas in Indigenous territories, and to how all these elements may contribute to conflicts. Our research identified two major structural flaws that have a direct impact on local conflicts related to oil and gas projects: poor subnational governance and gaps within legal frameworks. The following sections focus on the mechanisms that lead to conflict in the presence of these two major structural imperfections. The analysis also looks at how the presence of domestic structural flaws has indirectly contributed to the development of an increasingly solid Inter-American legal framework to address hydrocarbons conflicts.

POOR SUBNATIONAL GOVERNANCE

Improving institutional performance and governance is essential for breaking the cycle of conflicts related to natural resources, particularly when the upgrading leads to a better distribution of revenues and provides a sense of security and justice. It would not be totally accurate to associate Latin America's oil-related conflicts solely to an inequality gap caused by an uneven distribution of education, income, land, and political participation. The action, or inaction, of the state, certain political decisions, and misspending also contribute to the building up of resentment (Reid 2007, 124–58).

Very often, oil conflicts occur as a result of governance imperfections at the local level that affect the redistribution of oil revenues and the choice and subsequent implementation of local investment projects to benefit local communities. Poor procurement procedures, for example, ultimately jeopardize the use of oil revenues that should be available for sustainable community-development projects. This, in turn, results in conflict and discontent when the local population fails to enjoy the benefits of the oil projects being developed in their territories.

Governance inefficiencies in Latin America may be linked to the fact that democracies are still young and that the institutional improvements necessary for the democratic system to work effectively are, with a few exceptions, at an early stage of development. According to the well-known journalist Michael Reid, who specializes on Latin America,

> Latin America has made much progress in the past few decades. A sense of
> perspective is important: two generations ago a majority of Latin Americans

lived in semi-feudal conditions in the countryside; little more than a genera-
tion ago, many were being murdered because of their political beliefs. . . . The
relatively disappointing record of many of Latin America's democratic governments should be judged realistically against the scale of the problems that
they have had to face. . . . Progress has started to get the upper hand. Consolidating it requires incremental reform. . . . It also requires patience, hard
though that is to muster in the face of poverty. (2007, 310–15)

The fiscal decentralization process the three countries under study engaged
in was aimed at surmounting the obstacles that prevent an equitable distribution of oil revenues among regional and local governments. Instead, the decentralization attempts often served either to highlight governance problems present at local or regional government levels or to transfer inefficiencies from the
central government to the regions or localities where the oil or gas projects were
taking place. In the end, these structural flaws got in the way of a successful fiscal decentralization.

Decentralizing Inefficiencies

With democratization came decentralization, as many new democracies tried
to leave behind the highly centralized government policies of the past. Colombia was the first to adopt revenue decentralization in 1986, followed by Ecuador in 1997 and Peru in 2002. The process has been most successful in Peru, although the system still needs much improvement. In the case of Ecuador, when
President Rafael Correa took office in 2007, he retracted some of the fiscal decentralization policies of the past to allow for more control of oil revenues by
the central government.

   The following analysis of fiscal decentralization focuses on the Peruvian
case, but most of the findings are common to the other two countries and to
most other Latin American scenarios, for that matter. In Peru, subnational governance flaws prevented effective fiscal decentralization and eventually resulted
in conflict. Lima has been exemplary in redistributing natural resource revenues to the producing regions as part of the revenue distribution policies introduced by the Canon Law passed in 2002.[1] In spite of that, the distribution
of oil and gas revenues to the producing regions remains incomplete and is the
source of many conflicts. The Canon Law stipulates the transfer of a percentage of the oil and gas revenues from the central government to the local and re-

gional governments of the producing regions. The transfer varies from region to region and is calculated as a percentage of production volumes and prices. As Peru established itself as a natural gas producer and exporter, revenue flows to the producing regional and local governments increased significantly in the past decade. Between January and June 2010, Canon transfers to producing states went up by 65.2 percent, compared with the same period in 2009 (Ministry of Economy 2013).

Graph 10 shows revenue flows to Peru's five main producing departments between 2004 and 2010. Cusco, home to the Camisea giant natural gas deposits, experienced the most significant revenue increases: from 89,000 to 1,140,000 million Peruvian soles. Cusco normally gets 58 percent of total hydrocarbons revenues.

Oil and gas revenues are normally aimed at financing local social and economic development projects in producing regions. The Canon redistribution is also a way of compensating producing areas for the negative externalities caused by oil and gas development. An analysis of subnational government accounts shows that Peru has generally succeeded in materializing the actual transfer of oil and gas revenues to the regional and local governments of producing states. This is an important achievement in Latin America, a region historically characterized by strong central government control of natural resource revenues.

GRAPH 10   Peru: Oil and gas revenue distribution by producing region

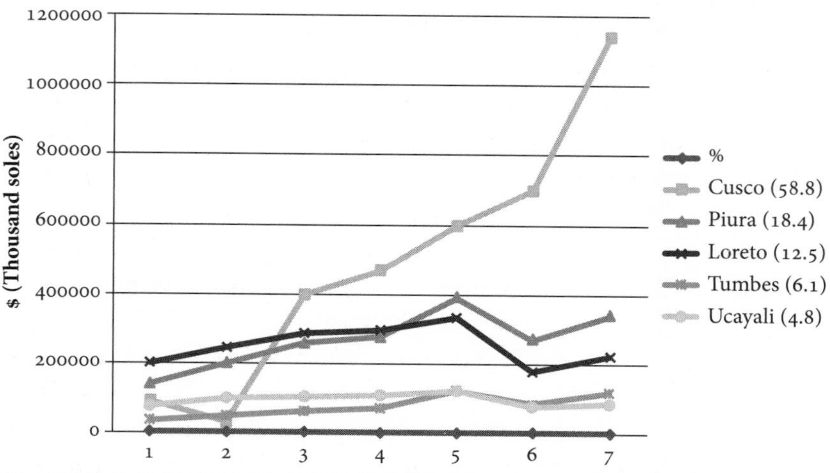

Source: Compiled by the author with data from Perupetro (2004–10).

However, once the oil and gas moneys are transferred to the regions in Peru, there are usually two possible scenarios that ensue. One scenario is a confrontation among producing regions, which start to compete for the funds. The second scenario is characterized by inefficient allocation of the new oil and gas resources once they arrive at the local or regional government levels. In both cases, there is bound to be conflict. Under the first scenario, the distribution of oil and gas revenues determined by the Canon Law is often asymmetrical and creates competition among producing regions for access to the new funds. By way of example, in 2008 the regional government of the department of Loreto, home to Peru's number one oil-producing field—from Blocks 1AB/8—received 51 percent of the Canon oil revenues (S$181 million soles), and the local producing regions of Loreto received 40 percent (PS$140 million). By comparison, that same year the regional government of another oil-producing department, Piura, received only 20 percent of the Canon revenues (PS$75 million), but the local governments there got the largest proportional share of all: 70 percent (PS$286 million) of the total (Perupetro 2010a). So in Loreto, where most of the country's oil is produced, populations living close to the fields received less revenue than those living close to oil-producing areas in Piura, where crude production is seven times lower. This uneven oil revenue allocation between regions and communities is a consequence of the way the Canon Law is designed. Local Indigenous populations living close to Loreto's Block 1AB/8 frequently occupied oil installations to protest this imbalance, which they considered unfair.

Another, perhaps more obvious, example of regional revenue imbalance that resulted in conflict is with regard to natural gas. In 2010 Peru became Latin America's first liquefied natural gas exporter with great fanfare, creating major expectations for the country to become a regional gas hub. But the excitement failed to reach the population of the district of Echarate, located in the province of La Convención, a few kilometers from the Camisea gas reserves. To the contrary, people in La Convención took to the streets for weeks in opposition to the liquefied natural gas exports, for fear the country's ample gas reserves would be exported without their reaping much in the way of benefits (Peru21 2002).

The population of La Convención had reason to be skeptical. In spite of living next to the huge Camisea gas reserves in the Cusco region, they could not afford to buy gas and they had to use wood for cooking (La República 2011). The pipeline for bringing gas at competitive prices from the nearby giant Camisea gas field to La Convención was still not installed because the attention had been focused on building the more profitable export infrastructure first. The daily reality of the inhabitants of La Convención contrasted with a much-publicized economic bonanza for neighboring Cusco, which received almost 60 percent of the total gas Canon transfers.

After two weeks of violent street demonstrations that left around twenty people injured, protesters in La Convención asked to talk to the country's prime minister himself and presented him with a laundry list of demands that went beyond mere access to the new gas reserves (*El Comercio.pe* 2010b). What emerged from their demands were old grievances that had not been properly attended to and, most important, a feeling of injustice among the local population who felt they would be the last ones to enjoy the promised bonanza of the Camisea gas, if indeed they received it at all.

Revenue data for Camisea shows that gas production and subsequent exports have contributed to Peru's impressive economic growth of the past decade (*Gestión.pe* 2011). Between January and October 2010, total oil and gas revenue transfers from Peru's central government to the regions were up by 47.43 percent (to PS$1.3 billion) from the same period in 2009. The fact that people living close to the country's—and one of Latin America's—largest natural gas reserves could not enjoy its benefits became a symbol of the difficulties in allocating natural resource revenues at the local level and opened up questions about the process of decentralization.

The second scenario of flawed fiscal decentralization is characterized by the presence of obstacles that get in the way of an equitable distribution of new oil or gas funds among the local or regional population. We have identified at least three such obstacles at the subnational level: the incapacity to locally administer increasing natural resource revenues, corruption and clientelism, and arbitrary political decisions due to lack of accountability of the local authorities.

The Ministry of Finance of Peru has gone a long way in trying to establish a system to select locally designed development projects to be funded by hydrocarbons revenues. But rigidities within the selection mechanism itself often result in the mismanagement of hydrocarbons revenues by local or regional governments. Locally designed development projects must be presented for approval to the National System of Public Investment (SNIP), where they are examined according to a set of preestablished criteria and requirements. Project approval by SNIP has been gradually decentralized, and since 2007 the evaluation of investment projects has almost entirely been done by regional and local governments. But the project criteria and its approval process remain highly demanding and intricate, which presents a major initial challenge, because local and regional governments often lack the know-how to successfully meet those high demands. The result is that many projects remain in the subnational SNIP pipeline without ever being implemented.

Efforts to solve these subnational rigidities have been generally unsuccessful for various reasons. One, reported by the Peruvian Office of the Ombudsman, is the existence of legal barriers to the transfer of human technical resources from the central to regional governments, due to the incompatibility of labor laws at both these levels or for lack of the necessary regulations for making the transfer effective (Office of the Ombudsman 2009b).

The other side of the coin is that a relatively demanding mechanism for the approval of investment projects, such as Peru's SNIP, may help to prevent corruption. The system calls for the involvement of technical experts to perform the required economic and social impact analyses of investment projects funded with natural resource revenues. This makes the process more transparent, as more people are involved. But, most important, a system thus conceived helps to spread the responsibility for deciding how to spend public funds beyond the realm of corruptible politicians.

However, this mechanism does not offer a total shield against a second type of assault that prevents the correct handling of oil resources by local and subnational governments: the presence of populist and clientelistic political dynamics. This behavior, particularly obvious in rural areas, prevents oil and gas funds from being properly and fairly invested and may lead to improper behavior. Given the highly demanding system for approval of investment projects under SNIP, and in light of poor accountability mechanisms, local authorities may be tempted to circumvent the official approval process and make arbitrary project decisions in an effort to achieve personal benefits or support political allies.

Corrupt or clientelistic actions may go hand in hand with a third hurdle preventing the sound allocation of hydrocarbons resources: arbitrary or politically influenced decisions to choose one investment project over another. Many investment projects presented by natural resource–producing regions aimed at nonproductive activities, such as embellishing public areas or building sports facilities, tend to pass the demanding SNIP requirements relatively easily, while other more pressing ones seem to get trapped in the system.

Clearly, political discretion functions in deciding which projects get funded and executed and which do not. The oil-rich regional government of Loreto, in Peru, was accused by the opposition in 2010 of failing to fulfill its promises in terms of investments that directly improved the livelihood of the population

(*La Voz* 2010). Most of the funds available had been earmarked for infrastructure projects, mainly road improvements and construction, which were seen as a priority for improving communications in this remote department. But at the same time, less than 40 percent of the population of Loreto had daily access to drinking water, 30 percent of children younger than five suffered from malnutrition, and only 45 percent of the population seventeen to twenty-four years old finished high school or a higher level of education (*El Comercio.pe* 2010a). Infrastructure projects are no doubt necessary, but at the end of the day, it is health, education, and access to basic needs that people take into account when judging their general living standards. The Loreto example shows a trend in Peru, where subnational governments of hydrocarbons-producing departments normally fail to apply participatory and transparent methods for designing development programs. The Loreto case also opened up questions about the accountability mechanisms in place for regional and local authorities with regard to investment decisions.

The seemingly arbitrary selection of projects with regard to their impact on the concerned communities indicates that there is more to the inefficient allocation of hydrocarbons resources than lack of know-how or capacity at the local or regional levels. At this stage the problem is one of political will and alliances, which becomes more obvious when certain flashy development projects are funded in lieu of other, more subtle ones that could nonetheless benefit a larger or more needy portion of the population but that lack political backing.

Corruption, nepotism, and clientelism in project investment decisions at local and regional government levels are some of the most common complaints among local communities coexisting with oil or gas projects. The more remote the communities, the less likely they will benefit from a clientelistic system, because they have limited connections to the minority who monopolize local power and gain from glitches in the system. People who perceive this reality experience a feeling of unfairness and frustration that often leads to conflict. A study of complaints received from local populations in fifty-six municipalities, conducted by the Peruvian Office of the Ombudsman, concluded that people blamed the municipal government to a much larger extent than they did the central government for governance irregularities and corruption (Office of the Ombudsman, 2008b). Among the main irregularities the research found were unauthorized municipal fees for the installation of drinking water networks, for parking, and for the opening of commercial outlets.

At the local level, corruption, nonresolved grievances, and lack of transparency in the management of oil revenues can easily ignite discontent. Indigenous communities in Ecuador's northeastern Sucumbios and Orellana departments occupied oil installations in 2002 to protest news that municipal representatives had received bribes for approving the construction of the oil-receiving Amazonas Terminal in their territory (Barthelemy 2003). This terminal is the starting point of the Oleoducto de Crudos Pesados that carries crude from the Amazon to a maritime terminal located in the province of Esmeraldas, on the Pacific coast. After weeks of protests that resulted in several dead and wounded, the government managed to reduce the level of the conflict by finally attending to some of the long-standing basic demands of the local communities. Construction of the oil terminal proceeded as planned.

Sometimes, illegal armed groups may try to capitalize on discontent in remote production areas. There are reports in Peru that the illegal armed group Shining Path, which was practically dissolved in the 1990s, is showing some isolated activity (SDPnoticias.com 2009). In 2003 the Shining Path kidnapped seventy-one workers from a firm building the Camisea natural gas pipeline in the Amazon jungle. Then in 2010, when farming and Indigenous communities called for street demonstrations to protest government plans to export gas from Camisea, the government said the demonstrators had been infiltrated by the Shining Path.

Much as in Peru, Colombia's fiscal decentralization failed to achieve an equitable distribution of oil resources and was tainted by very similar flaws, including the lack of regional and local capacity for making an intelligent allocation of the new resources. Most important, what hindered the success of Colombia's revenue decentralization was the ingrained corruption and clientelism that, as in Peru, continues to dominate the subnational government scenario, where the exchange of political loyalties for favors remains strong.

Colombia's oil revenue distribution system, set up by titles 11 and 12 in the 1991 National Constitution, had mixed results. The intent of the constitution in establishing the royalty transfer system was that the new funds would improve the capacity of subnational governments to invest in local development programs. Local and departmental governments followed that constitutional mandate and started to direct substantial new spending to education and health (Partow 2002). Interestingly though, none of the three main oil-producing departments, which received the bulk of the oil royalties, managed to meet the minimum goals set by law of reducing child mortality and expanding health, education, and drinking water coverage.[2] In 2010 Colombia was debating a controversial new royalty bill aimed at a more equitable distribution of oil royalties among producing and nonproducing states. The proposal stirred much opposition, as many in producing departments felt their share of oil revenues would be unfairly reduced with the new law (*El Espectador* 2010).

The decentralization process in Colombia did succeed somewhat in improving the accountability of local and regional governments for the use of hydrocarbons revenues and in developing participation mechanisms outside of the capital cities. But continued interventions by the central government in subnational investment decision making became a stumbling block in the process. The corruption of local politicians usually results in a misallocation of government moneys, and it is one of the main arguments used by the central authorities to keep tighter controls on subnational expenses. But the ongoing violence in Colombia, which prevents the development of good governance practices at subnational government levels, has made local and regional allocation of oil resources there uniquely difficult to implement (Velázquez 2003, 127–75). Many political leaders have been assassinated for trying to modify the old style political clientelistic behavior. Furthermore, fiscal decentralization in Colombia clashed with efforts by the central government to increase its presence in the provinces to improve its control over the country's long-lasting illegal armed groups.

In the case of Ecuador, starting midyear in 2000 the country has engaged in a process of recentralization, by which the distribution of oil resources has increasingly been placed back under the control of the government. The Organic Law for the Recovery of the Use of Oil Resources That Belong to the State, and Administrative Rationalization of the Debt Processes (no. 308), passed in 2008, cancelled two of three existing oil funds that previously distributed hydrocarbons revenues among producing provinces. Two years later article 94 of a new Hydrocarbons Law (no. 244) introduced a centrally managed distribution mechanism for oil revenue profits, by which 3 percent went to oil workers and 12 percent to the state. The funds were to be equally distributed among subnational producing regions for the funding of health and education projects. Unused funds would be reallocated for development projects in areas of the Amazon without oil. In addition, the two state oil companies (Petroamazonas and Petroecuador) would invest another 12 percent of profits in social and sustainable development projects throughout the country, and more specifically in poor oil-producing areas of the Amazon inhabited by Indigenous populations. There, the government planned to build new health centers, sport facilities, drinking water networks, and other infrastructure projects. The government announced in 2011 an initial distribution of US$350 million among Amazon populations living in oil-producing regions (Ministry of Nonrenewable Resources 2011a).

Fiscal decentralization was initially aimed at a more just distribution of hydrocarbons resources by allowing funds to make their way back to the producing regions. But in so doing, the process transferred to the local level some of the hydrocarbons revenue dependency and governance problems that usually plague the central governments of producing countries.

In the cases analyzed here, institutional weaknesses are present at the subnational government levels of the producing areas, which experience similar problems as central governments in handling oil revenues. The decentralization process thus transfers to subnational government levels not only oil revenues but also the flaws of the central government in managing them. Describing a similar relocation of governance flaws from a weak central state to even weaker regional and local governments in the case of mining, some authors have referred to the process as a new form of Resource Curse (Arellano-Yanguas 2008).

The concentration of income tends to reduce transparency and increase corruption because the new moneys are usually managed by a specific government agency or individual. In Peru that dependency is increasingly present at the regional and local levels, as the Canon revenue becomes the main source of income for most of the producing regions. In many cases the increasing role of the private oil or gas company as generator of social welfare without alternative sustainable economic development activities for the local population creates another level of dependency, in this case on the company.

It is at the subnational levels where oil dependency, weak governance, clientelism, corruption, and lack of know-how can be fundamental engines for advancing most of the local conflicts that characterize Latin America's oil and gas scenario today. Another key factor in that respect is the lack of strong state presence at the local level and weak communication between the central government and subnational authorities.

Weak Local State Presence and Imperfect Government Communications

In the Peruvian context communications between the central, regional, and local governments often tend to be poor and rather conflictive. It is not uncommon for the local government of the area where the hydrocarbons developments will take place to be unaware that the central government has granted a license to develop oil locally. Most oil and gas projects are signed off on by the central government, with little information provided to the region, municipality, or community prior to signing the contract. But when company activities start on the ground, the central government is usually absent, with the exception of limited mandatory consultation processes. This government void helps to undermine any sense of citizenship for the local population.

Local governors sometimes take the side of communities in opposing specific hydrocarbons projects, sometimes in reaction to grudges born from miscommunication with the central government, but often for political reasons. Conflictive or insufficient communications between the central government and its local agencies serve to create confusion about the role and responsibilities of each government agency and cast doubt on the legitimacy of the central government in its relationship with the population.

One of the main complaints of local communities affected by hydrocarbons projects is the lack of state presence in their territories, which are usually remote or neglected areas far from the capital city, where most decisions are made. The absence of the state in remote areas means that oil companies often adopt the responsibilities of the government as providers of basic services, particularly when there are no local development plans in place. In exchange for becoming the main provider of goods and services, the oil company demands community consent to carry out its operations in their territory. A direct relationship is established between the company and the community throughout the duration of the license, which can be for twenty-five or thirty years. Companies and communities set up a permanent negotiating process that generates a sort of bargaining momentum by which the community makes demands and the company responds with counteroffers. The whole process has very little government involvement. This modus operandi between private entities, devoid of a legal framework and with the absence of the state, often ends in conflict.

Often, the government—be it federal, regional, or local—takes a secondary role, as facilitator of the negotiations between the communities and the companies. This hands-off approach by the government is partly the result of laws that normally leave the responsibility for the design of community relations plans to companies. In the eyes of local communities, the government is relinquishing its responsibilities as provider of basic services and infrastructure. As an outsider, it is common to hear local Indigenous communities complaining about the fact that the state fails to protect their cultural and other interests from the oil company. In fact, they usually say the state is "on the side of the company." This opinion is reinforced by the fact that after years of neglect, the central government makes an appearance in their territory only prior to the development of the new oil project, but hardly ever before that. At that point, government officials organize formal consultations with Indigenous communities, as mandated by the law, and they are often accompanied by company officials. When there is a conflict with the company, local communities almost invariably demand that the government mediate as the only guarantor of agreements. The lack of effective and active central government presence at the local level is usually a major structural factor that contributes to conflict. Added to that, Indigenous Peoples feel they have a right to own the lands they have inhabited for centuries, with little or no government attention, at least not until oil or gas was found.

GAPS WITHIN THE LEGAL FRAMEWORK

Oil and gas legislation in Latin America tends to be diffuse and overlapping. There is an overabundance of laws that are not always applied harmoniously to solve specific problems, and often the problems are overlooked for political reasons. In many cases, various laws apply to a single matter and may differ on the extent of their application and on the rights they grant.

The lack of well-crafted, long-term national hydrocarbons policies aimed at setting priorities and parameters for the development of oil and gas in Latin America is a major source of inefficiencies. These priorities and parameters should preferably be within the existing legal framework and in accordance with national, regional, and local development and territorial plans. Well-planned hydrocarbons policies are usually not spelled out because, generally, they simply do not exist. Elements of hydrocarbon policies can be found in bits and pieces in various documents, but they do not constitute efficient guiding principles for the various stakeholders. In Peru and Colombia, governments have been focused mainly on attracting investments to the oil and gas industries in the past decade, seemingly as an end in itself rather than a means to achieve larger goals determined by the countries' development needs and priorities. In Ecuador the prevailing hydrocarbons policy during the decade was more focused on increasing the control of the state in oil operations, again as an end in itself, rather than a means toward larger goals for the society as a whole.

In this context the laws are not structured around specific goals stated as hydrocarbons development objectives, and they are rather a collection of independent, largely unconnected rules. Important constitutional premises are put to the test in the presence of oil-related conflicts. Some of the most controversial ones are the notion of "national interest" and the definition of ownership of subsoil resources. Often, the resolution of hydrocarbons conflicts gets delayed when the constitutional concepts are challenged in court, giving way to a myriad of legal interpretations and actions.

Very often the resolution of oil and gas conflicts lies in the hands of international tribunals, when affected populations who cannot find answers at home seek legal resolution to their grievances abroad. This has led to the development of international jurisprudence that frequently goes beyond the reach of domestic laws and sometimes forces their evolution. In the particular case of Colombia, even the existence of a uniquely well-developed body of law, relative to its neighbors, did not necessarily contribute to protecting the rights of Indigenous groups that were affected by oil and gas projects.

Exceptions to the legislation, confusion as to which laws apply when, and a loose interpretation of the law to accommodate oil blocks are some of the causes of constant conflict. The paradoxical situation of allowing oil projects in legally protected natural reserves or in Indigenous territories triggers great resistance from the environmental and the Indigenous movements. Ecuador and Colombia are the most striking examples of what Guillaume Fontaine (2007a) calls "State schizophrenia," a confusing policy that calls for environmental protection of specific areas while at the same time allowing for the expansion of the oil frontier within those zones. Ecuador's Yasuni National Park is a perfect example of this back-and-forth around the legislation on natural resource management, because throughout the years its borders were often expanded and then reduced again to accommodate oil projects. Seven oil blocks are within the borders of Yasuni Park (Blocks 14, 15, 16, and 17), plus the Ishpingo, Tiputini, and Tambococha area, which is thought to hold Ecuador's largest, still undeveloped hydrocarbons reserves (around 1.2 billion barrels of heavy crude). In the 1990s the size of Yasuni Park was reduced to leave Blocks 16 and 17 outside of its boundaries. At the same time, the territory of the Huaorani Indigenous groups living within the park was expanded, and land titles were granted.

In Colombia an attempt at establishing more comprehensive protection of natural reserves resulted in the creation of a dual system of national parks in the 1960s and of Indigenous protected areas (*resguardos* in Spanish) in the 1990s, particularly in the Amazon.[3] However, territorial conflicts erupted when the limits of the newly created protected areas were constantly redesigned to accommodate hydrocarbons projects, particularly in lands inhabited by Indigenous communities. The longest and best-known such conflict is with the U'wa Indigenous Peoples, in the Samore Block (later renamed Siriri and Catleya), located on the border between the departments of Norte de Santander and Boyaca. The long history of the conflict in U'wa territory is marked by a constant renegotiation of the limits of the Indigenous protected area and reserve to allow for oil development. Much of the dispute was in relation to the area where the Gibraltar 1 well was located, which the U'wa claimed was within their protected area.

In the case of Peru, by some accounts, more than twenty oil blocks are located inside some of the sixty natural reserves that spread throughout Peruvian territory (Calle Valladares and Brehaut 2007, 16–21). Some forty oil blocks were superimposed on the territories of Indigenous communities between 2003 and 2008, with four (Blocks 88, 110, 113, and 138) located in areas inhabited by Indigenous Peoples in voluntary isolation (Gamboa, 2009). This situation exists in spite of specific legislation that gives certain rights to voluntarily isolated Indigenous groups.

The source of these constant legal changes and confusing interpretations of the law may be found in two premises that characterize the legal systems of Latin American countries. One is related to the definition of "national interest," and the other is the concept of ownership of subsoil resources as an indisputable prerogative of the state.

WHICH LAW APPLIES?

When confronted with the option of preserving a protected area or developing an oil or gas project, Latin American governments may opt for the concept of "national interest," defined as the interest of the majority of the population. When an area is labeled as being of "national interest," then all other laws or regulations pertaining to the protection or special status of the area become void. Surface owners may be liable to compensation, but they can hardly contest the subsoil in their land being exploited, if the state so decides. Examples of this situation abound.

In Ecuador's national parks, oil operations have been historically carried out under the veil of article 6 of the country's 1999 Environmental Law (no. 37 RO/245), which allows for the exceptional development of nonrenewable natural resources in fragile ecosystems or protected areas in response to a "national interest." The legislation calls for a prior economic feasibility study and an environmental impact assessment. Critics argue that article 6 is contrary to international treaties signed by Ecuador, which do not admit exceptions to the general rule of forbidding oil operations in protected areas (Crespo Plaza 2007).

In Peru the government declared oil and gas exploration in Block 67 to be of national interest in May 2009, in spite of an ongoing dispute about the existence in the area of Indigenous populations living in voluntary isolation, reflected in the passage in 2006 of the Law for the Protection of Peoples in Voluntary Isolation or in Initial Contact (no. 28736). In response, local Indigenous communities took over the installations of the oil company, Perenco. Then President Alan García and Perenco denied the existence of uncontacted peoples, based on findings by an Environmental Impact Assessment research team. However, individual anthropologists from the team contradicted the assessment and confirmed that they did believe this population existed. The Indigenous organization Asociación Interétnica de Desarrollo de la Selva Peruana (AIDESEP) filed a lawsuit at the country's Constitutional Tribunal, which was dismissed in June 2010.

The idea of "national interest" often clashes with the concept of minority rights or rights of Indigenous Peoples, which has been incorporated into the constitutions of the three countries. The imposition of the general concept of national interest to support the development of natural resource projects in biodiversity-rich areas or in Indigenous territories invariably leads to conflict. The concept of national interest reinforces the antagonism between the majority population and the population of Indian descent, as it puts forward the notion of "us the majority," mostly understood as encompassing people of Spanish descent, against the minority Indigenous population. The affected minority populations often join forces with combative environmental NGOs to get their arguments across.

To resolve these conflicts, legal systems throughout the region have often become creative and come up with new arguments to make a case for preventing the development of hydrocarbons. One such legal avenue was the creation of intangible zones inside already protected areas. No industrial developments are allowed in the intangible zones, to isolate and protect either biodiversity or Indigenous communities. On February 2, 1999, two intangible zones were created in Ecuador by Executive Decree 552: one in Yasuni Park, for the protection of the Tagaeri-Taromenane Indigenous groups living in isolation, and another one in the Cuyabeno Reserve. The measure was only partially effective, because the borders of the newly declared intangible areas were subsequently changed several times. Both these protected areas have been the center of an ethnic-environmental alliance, as local Indigenous groups joined forces with some of the most radical environmental NGOs to oppose oil developments.

To find a more permanent solution to the controversies created by having to choose between hydrocarbons and protected areas, in 2007 Ecuador came up with an innovative idea for harmonizing conservation and hydrocarbons development. President Correa proposed delaying exploration in the oil-rich Ishpingo, Tiputini, and Tambococha fields within Yasuni Park. In exchange, he demanded an annual payment of US$350 million from the international community for keeping the oil under the ground. In 2012 the proposal had yet to attract significant international interest.

Our research found ample evidence of conflict related to hydrocarbons and changes to legally defined borders. Disputes of this kind were particularly common in Peru and Ecuador, where most of the hydrocarbons developments are located in environmentally and socially protected areas of the Amazon region. Of the total number of case studies analyzed for this book in the three countries, more than half included disputes related to unclear or constantly modified legally defined territorial borders.

THE OWNER OF THE SUBSOIL

While the prerogative of the state to declare an oil or gas activity to be of national interest can be controversial, another, even stronger government privilege is at the heart of a large number of hydrocarbons-related conflicts in Latin America: the right of the state to administer and exploit the resources that lie in the subsoil, regardless of who owns the surface land. This constitutional provision differs markedly from that of the United States, where whoever owns the surface land also has rights over subsoil resources and is entitled to develop them for a profit.

The granting of ownership of the subsoil to the state is one of Latin America's most complex conundrums and the underlying source of most conflicts related to natural resources. The constitutions of Ecuador, Peru, and Colombia are no exception to those of the rest of the region in that they establish that the state is the only one with rights to develop underground natural resources. Subsoil resources are a component of state assets that must be developed in the name of public interest, according to the constitutions of these three countries.

The concept of subsoil ownership by the state creates inevitable conflict with

TABLE 4	Constitutional mandate by country
Ecuador	Article 408. Nonrenewable natural resources are a property of the State that is nontransferable, cannot be legally taken away, and cannot be seized, as are, in general, subsoil products; mineral and hydrocarbons deposits; substances that are different in nature from that of the soil, including those found in areas covered by territorial sea waters and maritime zones [and] including biodiversity and its genetic heritage and the radio electric spectrum. These goods may be exploited only with strict adherence to the environmental principles established by the Constitution. The State will participate in the benefits for the use of those resources. The amount of these benefits will not be less than those gained by the company that exploits them.
Peru	Article 66. Renewable and nonrenewable resources are part of the heritage of the Nation. The State is sovereign in taking advantage of them.
Colombia	Article 332. The State is the owner of the subsoil and the nonrenewable resources, notwithstanding the rights acquired and perfected by preexisting laws.

Source: Compiled and translated by the author with data from Ecuador's 2008 Constitution, Peru's 2002 Constitution, and Colombia's 1991 Constitution.

individuals or groups, such as Indigenous or farming communities, who claim to have ownership rights over whatever is on the surface of hydrocarbons-rich areas. The exploration and exploitation of the oil or gas in the subsoil will inevitably affect those who hold rights to the surface.

The constitutional view of natural resources is irreconcilable with the concept of territory for Indigenous communities, for whom the geographical space where they live constitutes part of their identity. When Indigenous Peoples demand rights to their land, they are not just referring to the delimitation of the borders of a piece of property; they are talking about the habitat that characterizes that space. For them, a land title protects not only a piece of property but also their identity, insomuch as it encapsulates the territorial elements they themselves identify with. In other words, the identity of a specific Indigenous population is determined to a large extent by the territory it inhabits so that a territorial title is not just that—it is also an "identity title":

Trees are human, fish are human, water is human . . . so if you pull down our trees, kill our fish or contaminate our water, you are killing human beings for us.[4]

When talking about the ownership of subsoil oil deposits, the atypical case of the Cusiana oil field, located in Colombia's Llanos foothills, inevitably comes to mind. Until a few years ago, several families living in the area were receiving a small share of the profits from the oil exploration. Their right to subsoil compensation, most unusual in Latin America, came as a result of land titles given to these families during colonial times. Once Cusiana reached its full potential in the 1990s and proved to be one of Colombia's largest oil fields, the issue of subsoil rights claimed by these families became contentious and was the object of several lawsuits that reached the highest tribunals in the country.

Following Cusiana, and as Colombia discovered large oil reserves that turned the country into an important regional oil producer, legislation was adopted to prevent future property claims by individuals. In 1969 Congress passed Law 20 (later made effective by Law 93 in 1993), which gave unquestionable ownership of subsoil reserves to the state. The law made an exception to this rule in the case of land titles granted before 1969 over land holding already discovered oil fields. But Cusiana was discovered much later, at the end of the 1970s, so the legal exception did not apply in that case, and private ownership of the area was rejected in 1994 by Colombia's Council of State (Nullvalue 1994). In fact, Colombia's large oil deposits were all found after Cusiana, so the ownership exception was never applied at all.

There have been various attempts at solving the dichotomy between property of the territory and of the subsoil through compensation agreements. In Peru, for example, the 1997 Law of Private Investment (no. 26505; modified by no. 26570) stipulates that the oil company must negotiate an agreement with the owners of the surface property that must be subsequently approved by the state. The owners of the surface property are entitled to financial compensation (*servidumbre*) for the development of subsoil natural resources in their land.[5] This mechanism also leads to conflict, however, because there is much disagreement about the amount of compensation. In Ecuador the consortium that built the Oleoducto de Crudos Pesados (OCP) had to negotiate a right of way with each of the communities and individuals living along the five-hundred-kilometer length of the line. Differences over the amount of the compensation and environmental concerns raised by the OCP's route across the Mindo-Nambillo forest resulted in serious popular unrest and led to a strike in the departments of Sucumbios and Orellana in 2002. The government had to declare a state of emergency and threatened to expropriate the land along the OCP route if the parties involved in the dispute failed to reach compensation agreements. The authorities argued the OCP was of national public interest, which would justify the expropriations, as contemplated by articles 4 and 91 of Ecuador's Hydrocarbons Law, passed on July 27, 2010. In the end, only 1 percent of the land crossed by the OCP had to be expropriated for lack of compensation agreements, according to OCP representatives.[6]

The arbitrary interpretation of the law, its weak implementation, and the fact that it can be easily modified to accommodate specific needs has led affected populations over the years to seek alternatives abroad to solve their conflicts. This reality contributed to the development of an increasingly dynamic Inter-American legal system that for the past two decades has become ever more active in conflicts related to extractive industries. Inter-American courts have steadily become an increasingly influential instrument for shaping the domestic legal systems of Latin American countries, particularly when Indigenous Peoples are involved.

INTERNATIONALIZATION OF LOCAL CONFLICTS

Besides legal contradictions and overlapping legislation, there is sometimes poor capacity or simply a lack of willingness on the part of national judicial systems, particularly local courts, to resolve certain hydrocarbons-related conflicts. When the domestic legal and institutional framework is too slow, fails to provide answers to demands, or is corrupted, the population affected by an oil or gas project may resort to the courts in the home country of the foreign oil companies involved or to international tribunals. In the first case, legal cases filed in the oil company's home country follow legal provisions that allow for foreign nationals to sue companies that commit abuses overseas. In the United States, for example, the Alien Tort Statute (28 USC § 1350) allows U.S. courts to hear civil actions by foreigners for abuses committed by U.S. companies abroad (Drimmier 2010).

One of the best-known legal cases against a foreign oil company operating in Latin America, and the main topic of the award-winning Joe Berlinger documentary *Crude: The Real Price of Oil*, is the class action suit against Texaco for allegations of environmental damage in Ecuador. The lawsuit, which set a trend for multimillion-dollar legal actions against corporations for alleged social and environmental abuses, challenged the courts in both the United States and Ecuador. It was initially presented in a court in New York in 1993, where Texaco had its headquarters, but was relocated to Ecuador in 2003. The plaintiffs in the 1993 lawsuit alleged that Texaco dumped 18.5 billion gallons of toxic water in unlined, open-air waste pits that emptied into local rivers and streams. They claimed the toxins had negative effects on the surrounding ecosystem and on the health of the local population, mainly Indigenous Peoples. The twenty-year-old lawsuit, which had not yet been resolved in 2012, has attracted a great deal of attention through the years mainly due to the potential US$27 billion liability suit and the numerous allegations of corruption, government interference, illegal lobbying, and other such anomalies.

It is also common for oil-related lawsuits to be presented at international courts, such as the Inter-American Commission on Human Rights (IACHR) and the Inter-American Court on Human Rights, both independent tribunals created by the Organization of American States to defend human rights in the Americas. Historically, human rights were understood in the context of individual political or civil rights. But today, with the rapid development of the concept of cultural rights and of a specific body of rights that protects Indigenous populations, the definition of human rights has expanded to question government development policies inasmuch as these may constitute a threat to the physical and cultural existence of Indigenous Peoples.

This broader concept of human rights touches on the controversial issue of self-determination in the case of Indigenous populations affected by hydrocarbons. Self-determination, the right of citizens to control their own destiny, has been adopted by the United Nations Charter as one of its fundamental principles. Governments have been generally reluctant to fully recognize the extent of this principle for fear it would be understood as a right of populations to form independent, alternative, and autonomous states (Anaya 2005, 149–73).

The majority of the cases presented at the IACHR, which are analyzed in this book in the three countries under review, were primarily related to the rights of Indigenous groups to continue to live in isolation despite the discovery of hydrocarbons in their territories. The plaintiffs were Indigenous organizations or NGOs representing Indigenous groups living in isolation. There were three such cases in Peru, Blocks 39, 67, and 107, and two in Ecuador, Blocks 14 and 17. The discovery of oil or gas in areas thought to be inhabited by communities in isolation could put their livelihoods at risk. In the particular case of Block 39, the Supreme Tribunal of the department of Loreto, where the oil deposits are located, had ruled in favor of the oil company, stating that there was no evidence of the presence of uncontacted people in the area where oil and gas would be developed. This prompted the Indigenous organization AIDESEP to take the case to the IACHR. Similarly, the case of the U'wa Indigenous communities in Colombia, mentioned earlier, was presented at the IACHR when local courts failed to solve their grievances.

As the concept of human rights has become broader, the Inter-American system for the protection of these rights has adopted a more dynamic interpretation. Rulings by the Inter-American legal system in cases involving hydrocarbons and Indigenous populations are gradually becoming instrumental in shaping opinions and ultimately in influencing domestic law in Latin American countries. Probably the most innovative approach the IACHR has incorporated is related to the adoption of the rights of a group as a collective, as opposed to limiting rights to the individual, as has been traditionally the case. Of all the lawsuits presented at the IACHR in relation to Indigenous Peoples affected by extractive industries, three have reached the highest tribunal, the Inter-American Court, which handed down judgments that set important precedents.

The first case, *Comunidad Mayagna (Sumo) U'was Tingni v. Nicaragua*, involved the Awas Tingni Indigenous community of Nicaragua. On February 1, 2000, the Inter-American Court of Human Rights ruled that the state violated the right to property, granted by article 21 of the American Convention on Human Rights, to the detriment of the members of the Awas Tingni community. In an unprecedented ruling, the court stipulated that the state must take the necessary steps to delimit property and give titles to Indigenous communities based on their uses and customs. It was the first time an international tribunal with legally binding authority recognized that the right to Indigenous collective property had been violated when the state issued a logging concession.

The second emblematic case, *Comunidad Saramaka v. Suriname*, on November 28, 2007, involved a lawsuit by the Saramaka tribal community against the government of Suriname for failing to recognize their right to use and enjoy the natural resources within their traditionally owned territory. They argued this was necessary for their survival. The ruling was similar to that of the Awas Tingni in that it emphasized the right to collective land ownership on the part of the Saramaka. But the court went further by invoking the need for the state to engage in consultations and get the free, prior, and informed consent of the Saramaka for industrial development projects that could have major impacts on the population. The court ruling stipulated that the state must grant the Saramaka a collective title over their territory and must share with the local community the benefits derived from development projects. It also ruled that the Saramaka's right to land titles might be restricted by handing out extractive industry licenses in the area where they live, but only insofar as that restriction did not challenge the survival of the Saramaka as a tribal people.

In the third case, Pueblo Indígena Kichwa de Sarayaku v. Ecuador, the Inter-American Court issued a decision on July 25, 2012, in favor of the Kichwa Indigenous community of Sarayaku, located in Ecuador's Amazonian province of Pastaza (IACHR 2012). The Sarayaku Indigenous community had been opposed to oil operations in their territory since the arrival of the oil company Compañía General de Combustible in 1996. After a long series of legal rulings, the IACHR had given the Ecuadorean state until April 2010 to abide by its previous recommendations, which included the disposal of explosives left buried underground after seismic tests performed in 2002. The state did not comply with the commission's rulings, so the case reached the Inter-American Court.

The court ruling highlighted the importance of the process of free, prior, and informed consent in relation to natural resource projects with potentially negative effects on the local population. The Sarayaku ruling spelled out the elements of a successful consultation process by stressing the need for it to involve the local population from the very early stages of the conception of the extractive project rather than perform mere bureaucratic informative actions. The court ruling made the state responsible for the lack of a proper consultation process, which in turn resulted in violating the rights of the Sarayaku in favor of oil developments in their territory:

> The State is responsible for the violation of the right to consultation, to Indigenous communal property and to cultural identity, as granted by Article 21 of the American Convention, in relation to articles 1.2 and 2 of the said Convention, to the detriment of the members of the Kichwa Indigenous Peoples of Sarayaku.

> The State is responsible for having put gravely at risk the rights to life and to personal integrity, as recognized by articles 4.1 and 5.1 of the American Convention, in relation to the obligation to guarantee the right to communal property, as stated by articles 1.1 and 21 of the said Convention, to the detriment of the members of the Kichwa Indigenous Peoples of Sarayaku, in line with paragraphs 244 to 249 and 265 to 271 of this Sentence.

> The State is responsible for the violation of the rights to judicial guarantees and to judicial protection, recognized by articles 8.1 and 25 of the American Convention, in relation to article 1.1 of the said Convention, to the detri-

ment of the Kichwa Indigenous Peoples of Sarayaku, as stated by paragraphs 272 to 278 of this Sentence.[7]

The Court went even further by linking the lack of consultation with the loss of identity among the Sarayaku:

> The Court considers that the lack of consultation with the Sarayaku Peoples affected their cultural identity, because there is no doubt that the intervention and destruction of their cultural heritage implies a deep lack of due respect to their social and cultural identity, their customs, traditions, *cosmovisión*, and their life style, which naturally causes much worry, sadness and suffering among them.[8]

The Sarayaku ruling spelled out the obligation of governments to establish an early consultation process with local, affected populations, and it particularly stressed the need to respect the cultural and identity characteristics of the local populations. However, the court came short of granting the Sarayaku the right to ban oil developments in their territories, in line with the ILO Convention 169 right to consultation, which does not grant veto power to local communities. The ruling also served to reestablish the role of the regional justice system at a time when the Inter-American Human Rights Commission (IACHR), which presents cases at the court, was being challenged by its member states (*Economist* 2011).

The fact that the Inter-American Court focused its attention on three cases involving natural resource conflicts where Indigenous populations were affected shows the increasing significance this issue has within the Inter-American legal community. The IACHR stressed further the importance of this topic in a special report it published at the end of the 2010 session. In the report, the commission expressed concerns about the impact of natural resource developments on the livelihood of Indigenous groups, particularly in Peru and the other Andean countries:

> In its hearings and working meetings, the IACHR received very troubling information about some of the structural human rights problems that persist in the region, having to do with respect for the right to life and humane treatment, guarantees of due process and judicial protection, and the exercise of economic, social, and cultural rights. The IACHR is concerned about information it received regarding a number of issues, including . . . ongoing structural obstacles that hinder the effective enjoyment of Indigenous peoples'

right to their lands, territories, and natural resources, as well as the impact of energy and extractive industries that have been installed in their territories. . . . Moreover, in hearings on energy and extractive industry policies in Peru, and on the human rights of Indigenous communities affected by the mining industry's activities in the Andean region, information was presented on the existence of a broad development policy for extractive industries in the region, with no existing legal or institutional framework to protect the territorial rights and the participation of Indigenous peoples. (IACHR 2010)

The internationalization of legal proceedings has been one of the major weapons used by international NGOs and Indigenous federations for pressing their cases against indiscriminate oil and gas developments in Latin America. Having their cases presented at legal tribunals of Western nations or in Inter-American courts offered an international window to local conflicts and increased outside pressure on Latin American governments to respect Indigenous rights. This, in turn, contributed to the search for solutions to some of the conflicts involving Indigenous Peoples and helped to push large extractive industries to consider the adoption of more stringent safeguards.

But international attention also highlighted internal contradictions within the Latin American legal framework for dealing with natural resource conflicts. This is especially obvious when contrasting the strong "nationalist" legal code developed in the first part of the twentieth century to reinforce the prerogative of the central government as the unique representative of the nation, and the rapid evolution of laws in the past decade to protect minority rights, and promote decentralization and participation. In 2012 the role of the Inter-American legal system in solving cases of collective rights with regard to natural resources was being seriously challenged by its member states, which rejected numerous rulings by the IACHR in favor of Indigenous Peoples (Picq 2012).

LOCAL CONFLICTS AS GENERATORS OF DOMESTIC LEGAL TRANSFORMATIONS

Sometimes, hydrocarbons conflicts serve to accelerate the adoption of long-delayed legislation, usually after popular dissent succeeds in getting the attention of the authorities, or of society, to the grievances of a minority group. Often in such cases, passing new legislation to support the demands of the Indigenous population is a measure of last resort in response to violence.

The cases analyzed in this book are full of examples of bargaining mechanisms that eventually produce much-awaited legal changes. The fact that important legislation follows violent and sometimes deadly actions shows the limitations of democratic institutions to provide avenues for dissent and a general lack of attention to the conditions of Indigenous populations. After three years of grueling national debates on the issue, and with the Bagua confrontations still fresh in people's memories, in August 2011 Peru's Congress passed the Law of Previous Consultation that Indigenous Peoples had demanded for decades in relation to natural resources, particularly to hydrocarbons (*El Comercio.pe* 2011). Their demands existed in the framework of the ILO Convention 169 and the UN Declaration on the Rights of Indigenous Peoples, which stipulate that Indigenous Peoples must be consulted before developing natural resources in their territories. It was not until the deadly events of Bagua, which resulted in dozens of dead in 2009, that a consultation bill was finally sent to Congress (Kozak and Moffett 2009, A6). Until then, the right to consultation had been regulated in very general terms by the 2005 General Environmental Law (no. 28611).

Similarly laborious had been Peru's decision in 2006 to enact a nationwide legal requirement to treat waste water from oil operations by reinjecting it back into the reservoir. Passed by Supreme Decree 015-2006-EM, Regulations for Environmental Protection related to Hydrocarbons Activities also prohibits the dumping of contaminated production waters into ocean, rivers, and lakes. This requirement was passed only after decades of sometimes violent protests and the occupation of oil installations by Indigenous populations affected by oil projects in the Corrientes River in northern Amazon.

In Ecuador the legendary 1989 Sarayaku Agreements, signed with groups affected by oil operations in Block 10, located in the province of Pastaza, were instrumental in achieving legal recognition of territorial rights for these groups. The accords helped to reduce the intensity of the conflict, but only after years of resistance and sometimes violence. At first the government had rejected Indigenous demands for land rights, stated in a proposal presented by OPIP in 1990 — the Agreement on the Territorial Right of the Quichua, Shiwiar, and Achuar Peoples of the Pastaza Province, to Be Signed with the Ecuadorean State. But later the authorities yielded, following an Indigenous revolt in June 1990 and a huge march in 1992 — March for the Territory. The march covered almost four hundred miles, from Puyo, the capital of the oil province of Pastaza, to Quito, under the motto "For Earth, for Life: Let's revolt" (López 2004, 157).

The development of the conflict in Block 10 was unique. It resulted in the granting of long-awaited legally recognized territorial rights to Indigenous populations after decades of demands. As in Peru, the Sarayaku Agreements paved the way for the adoption of several nationwide laws: the Environmental Law of 1999, the Environmental Rules for Hydrocarbons Operations adopted in 2001, and the 2002 Rules for Consultation and Participation in Hydrocarbons Activities. For the Indigenous movement, passage of these national laws following Indigenous revolts may be seen as a victory. However, this process may have the unwelcome effect of serving to establish a perverse mechanism: the institutionalization of violent action as a way of achieving changes in policies or laws, particularly given the lack of well-established and functioning institutions to deal with popular dissent.

The Sarayaku Agreements themselves were reached as a result of negotiations for the liberation of a community-relations representative from the oil company ARCO. In exchange for his release, the Sarayaku Agreements called for the suspension of oil activities for a period of fifteen years in Indigenous territories. The moratorium was aimed at allowing time to develop a legal framework to address similar hydrocarbons-related conflicts in Indigenous territories. The agreements also called for the suspension of the process of granting new oil licenses in Indigenous territories, as well as immediate compensation for environmental damages caused during the exploration period. Once again, protest and coercion was the effective method used for forcing legislation regarding oil operations in environmentally and socially sensitive areas.

Similarly, oil conflicts forced the resolution of historical territorial claims by the Matses Indigenous community living in the Loreto region of Peru's northern Amazon. This group fervently opposed oil exploration in their territory beginning in 2007, when the government, ignoring their opposition, granted oil licenses to Pacific Stratus for Blocks 135 and 137 (*El Comercio.pe* 2008). The community was especially upset by the fact that the oil licenses had been issued in a matter of months, while their claim for the expansion of their territorial boundaries had existed more than a decade and still remained unresolved.

The Matses live in a national reserve, which under the Peruvian Law of Protected Areas (no. 26837), passed in 2007, allows for the commercial development of natural resources, provided a detailed management plan for the area is developed in advance. Around 3,000 community members live in the Matses National Reserve, of which some 1,700 are native Matses and 1,300 are newer groups, organized in farming communities. There are no roads to access the territory, and the only way of getting there is by plane or an hour-long boat ride from the town of Angamos. Blocks 135 and 137 are within the reserve, and they are said to be superimposed to the Reserved Zone Sierra del Divisor and the Isconahua Territorial Reserve (Martel 2010). Indigenous People in voluntary isolation are thought to inhabit the area, and to protect them organizations representing the Amazonian Indigenous Peoples have requested the creation of additional reserved areas—such as Yavari, Tapiche, and Kapanhua. The Matses argued that the state had failed to consult with them before giving the license to Pacific, so they refused to allow oil exploration in their territories. They opposed any kind of contact with either the government or the company and claimed that Blocks 135 and 137 were within a territory known as Tapiche Blanco, which they had unsuccessfully requested for years be elevated to the category of protected area.

Notwithstanding their opposition, plans for oil development in the Matses territory went ahead. The company tried to establish dialogue with the community, but with no success. The intervention of the office of the Peruvian ombudsman at the beginning of 2009 was key for bringing representatives from the Matses Peoples and the state-run oil company Petroperu, as well as officials from the regional and national governments, to a negotiating table. At the meeting, the Matses expressed their grievances and linked them to the lack of a strong government presence in their territories. They invited government officials to visit their lands and witness their living conditions. The official visit finally took place, and it was followed by much attention from the central government to the grievances of the Matses community, who specifically demanded better schooling for their children. The regional government committed itself to undertaking a study of the problems that affected the Matses community, with the idea of creating a development plan for the area.

By August 2009 the Matses Reserve, which originally extended to roughly 450 thousand hectares, was enlarged by another 420 thousand hectares and upgraded to the Matses National Reserve through Supreme Decree 014-2009. The territorial expansion came after fourteen years of futile requests by the Matses community, who had finally managed to turn the government's keenness in developing oil in their territories to their advantage.

For the Matses in Peru and the Sarayaku in Ecuador, who live far from their countries' decision-making capitals, external oil interest in their territory was the first opportunity they had to attract official attention to their grievances.

Renewed government interest allowed them to win historical territorial claims and to find resolution for some of their main difficulties. For Indigenous and environmental communities as a whole, hydrocarbons conflicts may ironically become useful tools for the materialization of long-awaited demands. These dangerous dynamics could result in the adoption of permanent conflictive situations as a means to an otherwise unobtainable end. In fact, some conflicts show elements that could lead us to conclude that Indigenous leaders, and some NGOs that defend their rights, have frequently engaged in this type of maneuvering. In these situations, conflict may become a permanent source of income for a few who engage in the protection of the rights of communities affected by oil or gas projects.

DEFINING WHO IS INDIGENOUS

Because the territory they live in is a defining element of the identity of Indigenous Peoples, land issues have always been at the top of their demands. The territorial rights of Indigenous communities have been gradually curtailed in Latin America over the centuries, particularly in relation to land use and ownership. This historical fact underlies all conflicts related to hydrocarbons developments and has become a recurrent complaint and a major source of grievance among Indigenous populations. A deeper examination of how Peru has historically treated land rights in relation to its Indigenous population offers some insights for understanding the growing number of natural resource conflicts in that country in the past decade.

The bloody Bagua confrontations of 2009 in the Peruvian Amazon were in reaction to government decrees passed that year that the Indigenous Peoples considered to be detrimental to their land rights. But in reality, the violence in Bagua could be understood as an expression of historical territorial grievances that date back to both Latin America's land reforms of the 1960s and Peru's constitutional amendments of 1993. During the Bagua events, protestors put forward two demands. One was for the restoration of land rights they lost in 1993. The second was related to the process of consultation and is analyzed more in depth in chapter 4. With regard to the first demand, Peru's 1993 constitutional reform canceled two land rights that Indigenous Peoples had historically enjoyed: the right to avert their lands from being sold (inalienable) and the right to prevent them from being used as a guarantee for credits (not seizeable). A third privilege historically enjoyed by Indigenous communities, which prevented others from putting a claim on Indigenous land, was partially reduced by the 1993 Constitution, which introduced the possibility for a third party or the state to claim territories that lie idle. The curbing of these three territorial rights had negative repercussions in Peru and beyond. In 1999 the United Nations Committee for the Elimination of Racial Discrimination expressed concern about the restrictions introduced by the 1993 Peruvian Constitution (United Nations International Convention 1999).

Added to the frustrations among Indigenous groups generated by the curtailment of their land rights was the lack of efficient territorial planning. None of the three countries analyzed in this book showed serious policies for demarcating the areas apt for industrial development and those that should be preserved due to their social or environmental characteristics. Land planning seemed to be more a function of the number of natural resource licenses they received, and not the other way around.

The restrictions to Indigenous land tenure introduced by Peru's 1993 constitutional reforms were not a new idea. Long before, Indigenous Peoples in Peru had been directly affected by the land reforms that spread throughout Latin America in previous decades. In the three countries under study in this book, land reforms created agrarian communities and gave peasants (*campesinos* in Spanish) access to land. This created an incentive for Indigenous Peoples in the highlands to register as campesinos to receive land (Yashar 1999). Within these agrarian communities, Indian ethnic origins were replaced with class affiliations and the word *campesino* replaced *Indian* (*indio* in Spanish) in the highlands. The word *indio* was used to refer solely to the Indigenous Peoples of the Amazon, who managed to keep their customs, beliefs, and access to land relatively intact because the large land and economic reforms of the past century impacted them less, due to their remote location.

Fear of being forced to assimilate like their highland ancestors is one of the main forces fueling hydrocarbons conflicts today among Indigenous Amazon populations. In Peru, where Indigenous groups are hardly recognized as such, that fear is even greater and may explain why that country shows the fastest growing number of hydrocarbons-related conflicts involving Indigenous Peoples. After the 2009 Bagua events, the International Labor Organization Committee of Experts on the Application of Conventions and Recommendations released an Individual Observation that echoed a similar document on

Peru it had produced in 1998. Both times, the committee emphasized an unresolved matter it considered to be key regarding conflicts in Peru: the lack of
a unified definition of Indigenous People (CEACR 2010, par. 4). Chapter 6 of
Peru's National Constitution recognizes only native and farming communities
(*comunidades nativas y campesinas*) but does not expressly mention Indigenous
Peoples. Other laws in Peru, however, do refer specifically to original peoples
(*pueblos originarios*) or Indigenous Peoples.

This lack of legal clarity and the quasi-denial of the existence of a distinctive cultural group may lead to confusion and frustration, as well as to potential
xenophobic reactions from radical groups within the population. Having various interpretations about who is, and who is not, Indigenous makes it difficult
to determine the extent of Indigenous legal rights and creates conflictive situations. This confusion was clearly illustrated in the arguments used by the Peruvian government as part of a collective lawsuit filed by five thousand people
in 2009 at the Constitutional Court. The plaintiffs alleged that they were not
consulted prior to the approval of one of the government decrees that led to the
Bagua events. In its defense, the state argued that the ILO Convention 169 did
not apply in the Bagua case because the Peruvian population is predominantly
mixed (*mestiza*) and thus no longer Indigenous. The state's line of reasoning argued that farming communities that were originally Indigenous became mes-
tizas with the development of civilization and, for that reason, granting them
the condition of Indigenous Peoples would be inappropriate (*Gonzalo* 2010).

The local Indigenous population understood the government's position in
the Bagua case as a denial of their identity and a continuation of the integration policies of the colonial period. The position of the authorities in this case
seemed to overlook the evolution of the Indigenous movement in the Peruvian
Amazon. There, the Indigenous movement has been strongly assertive of Indigenous identity in past decades and in so doing succeeded in differentiating
Indigenous Peoples from the historical assimilation process that characterized
the Andes. Acceptance of the existence of a differentiated ethnic group, in this
case Indigenous Peoples, would be the obvious starting point for granting legal
rights and obligations. Without that recognition, and without understanding
the relationship that minority group has with the land, conflicts regarding hydrocarbons in the territories Indigenous Peoples inhabit are bound to continue.

It is no surprise, then, that in the two countries in our study with the largest
Indigenous populations, Peru and Ecuador, most of the hydrocarbons-related
conflicts have involved Indigenous land disputes: sixteen out of twenty in Peru,

and nineteen out of twenty-three in Ecuador. In Colombia seven out of twelve conflicts analyzed involved Indigenous land claims.

EXEMPLARY CONSTITUTION, IMPERFECT SCENARIO

Colombia is quite the opposite of Peru with regard to recognizing ethnicity. As far back as 1991, Colombia reformed its constitution to bring in a new legal system aimed at addressing the country's deep inequalities and discrimination against minority groups. The reforms introduced a progressive constitutional legal system and a body of jurisprudence unparalleled in the region (United Nations 2010, 7). Some of the most innovative rulings contained in the new constitution concern the rights of Indigenous Peoples. Particularly revolutionary were the incorporation of customary law into the new constitution and the articulation of Indigenous laws in the legal system. The object was to make Colombia into a more pluralistic society and to set the country among the most advanced in terms of legislation to protect the rights of minority groups. Constitutional reform tried to achieve that aim from the start by including two Indigenous representatives from the country's largest Indigenous organizations at the Constituent Assembly that amended the constitution in 1991. This move was charged with strong symbolic meaning, as it meant the inclusion and acceptance by society of the most marginalized groups (Van Cott 2000).

The 1991 Constitution, through the introduction of the figure of *tutela*, allowed individuals to seek protection of their fundamental rights by an institution especially created to serve that purpose: the Constitutional Court. The process for presenting claims at the Constitutional Court is easily accessible by ordinary citizens, and so far it has produced relatively quick answers. Any individual may present a written or verbal claim in defense of his or her fundamental rights, through a simple process and without needing a lawyer (Delaney 2008, 50–59). The Constitutional Court then has ten days to rule on a tutela claim. This flexibility and ease of access allows the court to make quick rulings to defend the fundamental rights of the population, which in turn is key in reinforcing the legitimacy of the court among ordinary Colombians. The tutela has become very popular among Colombians, as demonstrated by the impressive increase in the number of cases presented at the Constitutional Court: in 1992 a total of 8,000 tutela judicial cases reached the court, and by 2005 there were more than 221,000 (Cepeda Espinosa 2006).

The government in Colombia generally respects the prerogatives of the judiciary, a rare circumstance in Latin America's largely clientelistic legal system. Also unusual is the fact that the highest courts of the country enjoy considerable standing and respect among the population, particularly the Supreme Court, the public prosecutor, and the Council of State, an advisory body of distinguished jurists. The Constitutional Court has the prerogative to challenge the legality of executive and legislative measures, and it often does. For example, in 2008 it declared unconstitutional a forestry law that had been passed by Congress in 2006, arguing that the new law had failed to conduct a prior consultation with affected communities, as required by the ILO Convention 169.

Many of Colombia's efforts have centered on the development of an exemplary constitutional system and ample jurisprudence to attend to social inequalities and to address the armed conflict that has plagued the country for four decades. In addition to the constitutional reforms, the government introduced numerous programs to protect vulnerable populations, such as farming or Indigenous groups, who live close to oil developments and are constantly harassed by illegal armed groups. A variety of government departments is involved in these programs, and there are also numerous special plans for attending to the needs of the internally displaced, for fostering respect for human rights among state armed forces, and for developing understanding of the specificities that characterize Indigenous cultures, among other minority groups.

Yet these programs, policies, and efforts have failed to effectively protect the U'wa Indigenous People that live in the department of Nariño from constant attacks by various armed groups. Despite a special government program geared at protecting the U'wa, following a 2009 visit by the special UN rapporteur, twelve U'was were killed, including women and children, and four hundred members of that ethnic group were displaced. The U'wa are particularly at risk because they live close to the Trasandino pipeline, which takes crude for export from the Amazonian department of Putumayo to the Colombian port of Tumaco by the Pacific Ocean. The Trasandino is the second most attacked oil infrastructure in the country after Caño Limón. Incidents of oil theft and illegal refineries along the length of the pipeline are permanently being reported by armed forces patrolling the area (*El Tiempo* 2011a). Farming and Indigenous communities living there, such as the U'wa, are regular victims of the armed conflict. They sometimes become human shields, or their local schools are turned into barracks by the fighters during armed confrontations.

An abundance of laws and policies is not necessarily enough to solve disputes related to vulnerable groups, as is obvious from the situation of the U'wa in Nariño. An observation by the Constitutional Court on government actions with regard to the forced displacement of Indigenous Peoples affected by the armed conflict asserts that reality:

> The answer of the government authorities to the critical situation that has been documented [in relation to the forced displacement of Indigenous Peoples affected by the armed conflict] has mainly been through the passage of norms, policies and formal documents, which in spite of their value, have had precarious practical effects. (*Protección* 2009)

In spite of Colombia's efforts to build well-respected judicial institutions and a body of laws to address the country's problems, serious institutional flaws and weak governance have prevented the system from excelling. A major problem is corruption, particularly within low-ranking judicial courts. Even the most influential figures have been accused of unlawful deals. In 2001 the prosecutor general, a political appointee, was charged with interfering with human rights investigations (Human Rights Watch 2002).

Laws can be difficult to enforce in areas where violence dictates the development of events and illegal armed groups seem to rule, such as in Nariño. The problem is even worse when institutions do not work effectively, or when they are corrupted to benefit a few. In this sense Colombia is an exception, where despite a very progressive legal framework and many government programs in favor of the Indigenous population, a lack of government control over its territory, plus armed violence and abuse, characterize the development of hydrocarbons and result in large losses of lands by Indigenous communities.

SUMMARY

This chapter examines some structural flaws that have been historically part of Latin America's institutional system and that often create the context for the development of oil and gas conflicts. Imperfections in Peru's fiscal decentralization process provide an example of major governance weaknesses that prevent oil revenues from reaching the local population and result in conflict. Another structural flaw common to the three countries studied in this book is related to unclear, overlapping, overlooked, or constantly modified laws. Weaknesses in the legal system are frequently a source of conflict in relation to natural resources, and particularly to oil and gas. This chapter provides various examples of laws that are constantly being modified to accommodate oil projects, leading to disputes.

Structural flaws in governance affect not only hydrocarbons but also mining and other natural resource sectors that have been the engine of Latin America's economic growth for the past two decades. Government resistance to finding lasting solutions to these structural flaws usually comes from a reluctance to accept that the multicultural nature of their societies creates differentiated visions of development, and that these need to be accommodated to avoid conflict. That reluctance is political in nature and exemplifies the fact that solving local oil conflicts calls for political decisions that go beyond the specific causes of the disputes. When addressing local hydrocarbons conflicts, it is important to keep in mind the sociopolitical and economic reality in which they occur, rather than treating them as isolated events.

CHAPTER 4

Transient Triggers of Local Conflicts

THIS CHAPTER ANALYZES the dynamics of a particular set of stressors that affect the intensity or the duration of conflicts. These conflict triggers are normally restricted to the physical region where the oil or gas is being developed and usually involve the stakeholders in the oil project. If left unattended these stressors may turn into important destabilizing forces. But in important ways they are different from the structural flaws described in chapter 3. These types of subnational triggers of local oil conflicts may be easier to address if tackled promptly, because they are more transitory and less embedded in the system. Sometimes, simple changes in the political or institutional context, or a modified approach to the dispute, may minimize their intensity.

Oil conflicts develop around the presence or absence of a variety of factors that may contribute to aggravating the dispute. Because local conflicts are very specific to the region or to the stakeholders involved, there is no one-size-fits-all solution. But local conflicts do share some common stress elements, which may or may not be all present at the same time but which do not require timely attention in order to reduce their intensity. Sometimes it is the absence of the fundamentals needed to resolve a conflict—such as proper institutional mediation—that prevents the prompt resolution of the dispute and becomes itself a stress factor.

Our research has identified four common local stressors of oil conflicts in the three countries examined: the level of radicalization or cohesion of the organizations involved in the dispute, the extent and nature of civil society involvement, the availability and efficiency of institutional mediation, and the strategies of oil companies for incorporating safeguards or for delivering services to the affected communities. Colombia presents a unique case due to the active guerrilla movement in that country, which is in itself an additional stressor, adding another dimension to oil-related conflict. For that reason, the case of Colombia is analyzed separately at the end of this chapter.

THE LEVEL OF POLARIZATION OR COHESION
OF THE ORGANIZATIONS INVOLVED

Our research shows that a unified Indigenous voice usually allows for a faster resolution of oil or gas conflicts. When Indigenous groups embrace a common cause and stand united behind it, they are more likely to be able to use the prevailing sociopolitical climate to their advantage and to engage in fruitful negotiations that result in long-term gains. However, when Indigenous federations or NGOs that represent them in the conflict are internally fragmented, the disputes tend to take much longer to resolve and can drag on for decades. The history of the development of Ecuador's Indigenous movement and the way in which it has coped with local oil conflicts is a good example of how an organized and unified alliance behind an Indigenous cause can achieve relatively rapid and substantial gains or solutions. By contrast, the lack of a unified Indigenous voice in Peru has led to fragmentation and increased conflict among Indigenous communities when they have been confronted with the threat of hydrocarbons developments in their territories.

Cohesion versus Division

In 1986 Indigenous groups from Ecuador's three main geographic areas—the coast, the mountains, and the Amazon—came together through the Confederación Kichwa del Ecuador (ECUARUNARI) and the Confederación de las Nacionalidades Indígenas de la Amazonia Ecuatoriana (CONFENIAIE) to create the country's largest indigenous umbrella organization, the Confederación de Nacionalidades Indígenas del Ecuador (CONAIE) (De la Torre 2006). Some researchers have argued that the single most important factor that led to the expansion of the CONAIE was increased oil development in the Amazon jungle, because many of the struggles the organization was involved in related to the negative externalities of oil exploration and production there (Sawyer 2004, 98–209).

Before the 1990s the environmental and social track record of oil companies went generally unnoticed in Latin America, particularly in remote oil-producing areas, in spite of the fact that major oil disasters in the region had started early on, in the 1970s, when large-scale oil operations began in the Amazon. Texaco drilled the first oil well in the Ecuadorean Amazon in 1967 in Lago Agrio, in the province of Sucumbios. The resulting contamination became a cause célèbre only decades later, mainly due to a lengthy—twenty year—ongoing lawsuit against Chevron (which later acquired Texaco). The company was charged a US$8.6 billion fine by an Ecuadorean court in February 2011 (BBC News 2011). Similarly, Occidental Petroleum started to drill for oil in the Peruvian Amazon province of Loreto in 1972. Evidence of social and environmental contamination in that area was found at the beginning of the 1990s but was not made public until several years later. It was not until 2006, when the Dorissa Accords were signed, that Pluspetrol, the company operating in the area, agreed to some of the demands of the local Indigenous population and to fund social projects for the affected population.

In Ecuador, oil exploration resumed at the end of the 1960s with the arrival of Texaco, after an interval of more than a decade of almost no significant activity. The oil boom that ensued in the 1970s and 1980s in the Amazon coincided with a growing drive, throughout the country and internationally, for recognition of an Indigenous voice and culture. An increasing focus on education and institutional development through capacity-building efforts led by international cooperation agencies, national and international NGOs, the government, and religious organizations produced a well-prepared and more aware Indigenous elite that emerged at the forefront of the active Indigenous movements of the 1990s. It was around that time that Ecuador's Indigenous Peoples began to acquire a larger presence in national politics by adopting the idea of a renewed pro-Indian movement (*neo-indigenismo* in Spanish). Rather than push for the integration and assimilation of Indigenous groups in society, this view promoted accepting the distinctiveness of their culture (Lara 2007, 175–206). This approach was largely supported by an international movement for the recognition and preservation of the Indigenous culture promoted by multilateral organizations—such as the World Bank, the Organization of American States, and the United Nations—through the adoption of safeguard policies for the protection of Indigenous populations.

Increased Indigenous activism coincided with the dissemination of public information in Ecuador—and also abroad—about the negative effects of oil developments in that country, particularly in the area developed by Texaco in Lago Agrio.[1] Indigenous groups used this momentum to their advantage and started to mobilize against oil developments. This process set the stage for the subsequent proliferation of oil conflicts, as Indigenous populations challenged oil projects by actively opposing them in their territories. The Indigenous cause was particularly successful in the conflict around oil developments in Block 10, located in the province of Pastaza. There, following a process of Indigenous empowerment, local communities represented by the Organización de los Pueblos Indígenas de Pastaza (OPIP) succeeded in obtaining a moratorium on oil exploration in their territories until land rights were officially recognized for Indigenous groups living in the area.

This unprecedented victory for the Indigenous movement came as a result of intense activism behind a common cause: the acquisition of land rights. Oil had become a tool toward that goal. It was around that time, in March 1990, that the largest Indigenous mobilization so far took place in Ecuador, with repercussions throughout the continent. Nationwide demonstrations supported by the CONAIE succeeded in elevating the Indigenous movement, which managed to make unprecedented gains in Ecuador. Indigenous leaders for the first time acquired national political status and accomplished their goal of turning the country into a multicultural state, an attribute that was enshrined in the 1998 Constitution. Another constitutional amendment that resulted from the 1990 Indigenous mobilization was the requirement that local communities be consulted before the development of any extractive industry activity in their territory. This concept became controversial due to differences in the interpretation of "consultation." Yet one more victory for the Indigenous movement in Ecuador was the abolition of the Agrarian Reform of 1964. Indigenous groups had opposed the reform for decades because they blamed it for legalizing the arbitrary seizure of their lands and facilitating the arrival of outsiders to their territories (Lara 2007).

This dynamic and organized Indigenous movement achieved unprecedented political activism and strength, so much so that it contributed to the ousting of two presidents, Abdala Bucaram in 1996 and Jamil Mahuad in 2000. The CONAIE was instrumental in the failed coup of 2000 against President Mahuad, in alliance with the military (Martinez Novo 2009). Most important for the Indigenous movement, CONAIE played a fundamental role in the 2002 electoral victory of President Lucio Gutierrez, who for the first time brought in (three) Indigenous ministers to his cabinet. Subsequent disagreements with the government resulted in the prompt dismissal of the Indigenous cabinet members, just months after taking office. The Indigenous movement became again oppositional, but this time with less force, as it started to lose its previous cohesiveness.

Unlike in Ecuador, Indigenous groups in Peru failed to come together from an early stage, most likely as a consequence of the political process that country was undergoing in the 1980s and the beginning of the 1990s. At that time Peru was immersed in a violent war against the Shining Path guerrilla movement. The armed conflict made it dangerous for Indigenous Peoples to protest or to gather in organized groups for fear of repression. In Ecuador, by contrast, indigenous protests were met with efforts at solving differences through dialogue rather than repression, which is part of the reason the Indigenous movement there was stronger (De la Torre 2006). It was not until almost a decade later that Amazon Indigenous groups in Peru became more vocal.

The majority of the cases we analyzed in Peru involved fragmented Indigenous organizations, a situation that delayed considerably the resolution of the hydrocarbons disputes that started to multiply after 2000. Our research found only one example in Peru of a relatively united Indigenous front, in relation to the conflict in Block 1AB-8. At one point, this dispute showed positive resolution, with nationwide effects. In Block 1AB-8a the unified northern Achuar Indigenous group achieved something thought unachievable in Peru: they managed to get the oil company Pluspetrol to agree to reinject contaminated waters, even though the law in Peru stipulated the need for such actions only for new oil contracts signed after 2005. The license for Block 1AB-8 had been signed in the 1970s, so Pluspetrol was under no legal obligation to reinject the waters, but the company gave in to unified Indigenous demands, including funding social projects for the affected population (Chiriff 2010).

The rest of the case studies analyzed in Peru showed a fragmented national Indigenous movement that resulted in conflict at the local level, when communities failed to show cohesion when confronted with the arrival of oil companies to their territories. This is best exemplified by the case of Peru's northern Amazon Block 64, which stretches through Indigenous Achuar communities that live in the Pastaza and Morona river basin. The initial concession for the area was granted to ARCO in 1995 and then transferred to Occidental Petroleum (Oxy). Both companies were forced to declare *force majeure* due to the hostility of the local Indigenous communities to their operations. Like in Ecuador, communities living around Block 64 were initially united in their opposition to oil operations, so much so that their consistent resistance resulted in Oxy leaving in 2007. The company that acquired Oxy's operations at that point, the Canadian Talisman, also inherited the conflict. In an effort to reduce the level of hostilities from local communities the new company engaged in the laborious job of meeting with each and every one of the Indigenous families living within its licensed area to negotiate their individual acceptance of its operations.

By the time Talisman arrived, the Indigenous communities of the area had seen their previously united front collapse, and the company's negotiating technique of acquiring one-on-one family approvals for its operations created new tensions and divisions among them. In the end, Talisman succeeded in getting seven Achuar families on its side, and by 2011 it was in negotiations with another five. The Achuar that approved of the oil operations hoped these would bring jobs that would in time help them improve their living conditions. But there were still some forty more families opposed to the oil project. Also unhappy were communities living downriver, who complained that polluted water from oil operations trickled down to where they lived. This added additional complexity to the conflict. Because of these overwhelming community divisions, Talisman was careful to make sure that new oil developments were located in the areas close to the communities that had agreed to the project.[2]

The Achuar were now openly divided vis-à-vis oil developments in their territory, and in May 2009 those living in the area of Block 64 nearly came to a confrontation. A group approached Talisman's headquarters and demanded to speak with a company representative to communicate their desire that the company leave. The group later claimed to have been confronted by other armed Achuars who supported company operations in the area.

> We are all Achuar, we are all brothers, but we are not well among each other now, we are restless, we don't talk well to each other. Before, we were happy people. Today some of our brothers don't welcome us because we are against the company. . . . What happened to us? We need to come back together again.[3]

The Peruvian ombudsman had to intervene and succeeded in getting a commitment from Indigenous representatives from the different factions to resolve their differences with Talisman through direct dialogue, rather than confrontation (*La República* 2009b). After that incident, the Achuar from the Pastaza and Morona river basins, with support from international NGOs, sent common representatives to a Talisman shareholder meeting in Canada in May 2010 to demand that the company abandon their territory. Talisman responded that it had restricted its operations to the areas upriver where local families had agreed to the oil project.

Local conflict is bound to continue in Block 64 and may expand beyond the project's borders, given its significance for Peru's economy. Block 64 is particularly important for Peru because it is one of the few areas where the intensive exploratory efforts of the past years showed considerable positive results. For

Talisman, Block 64 represented the best oil find of the five oil concessions the company held in Peru. Adjacent Block 101, also operated by Talisman, was also conflictive for similar reasons. The company set up its operations headquarters there between two communities—Soplin and Sabaloyacu—which until then shared the same territory. A conflict similar to that of Block 64 developed: Sabaloyacu agreed to allow Talisman in its territory, so the company set camp closer to this community, but members of Soplin were not happy. The two communities were now physically separated by company installations and philosophically opposed with regard to oil operations in their territory (Indigenous Peoples 2010). Talisman withdrew its operations from Peru at the end of 2012, after eight years (Reuters 2012).

Links with Umbrella Organizations

Communities affected by hydrocarbons developments are generally represented by grassroots organizations that operate in the remote territories where they live, close to the oil project. Sometimes, the communication channels between these grassroots organizations and their national counterparts are not very fluid, perhaps simply because of the distance between them. The end result is that often deals are made locally, without the knowledge or support of the umbrella organizations, whose leaders at the time may be more focused on building political alliances in the capital city or on raising international funds to support the Indigenous cause.

Local community leaders tend to understand the day-to-day problems of their members who live close to the oil or gas project. For that reason they are better placed for making concrete demands at the negotiating table with companies or governments, such as improving basic services or building much-needed infrastructure. The more grandiose goals of achieving political Indigenous participation at the national level or institutionalizing the rights of communities through legislation are normally sought by the more politicized national umbrella organizations.

When local and national organizations work in tandem, the results can be very positive. At the start of the conflict in Ecuador's Block 10, the Indigenous movement showed a high level of organization and professionalism in putting their demands forward and in keeping open communication channels with a large network of grassroots community organizations. It was to a large extent due to that outstanding structural organization that the historical Sarayaku Agreements were signed in 1989 between the Indigenous federations and the oil company. Following the agreements, and after some Block 10 communities succeeded in legalizing their territories in 1992, the regional Indigenous organization OPIP presented the government with an Integral Development Plan that included specific economic development goals for the area. The plan was the result of coordinated work between grassroots and umbrella organizations that showed a high level of cohesion throughout the Indigenous network. This process showed unprecedented nationwide gains for the Indigenous movement, including passage of new regulations on oil activities. The local population of Villano also benefited tremendously by receiving direct attention to their grievances, as well as a number of titles to their lands.

Unfortunately, in Ecuador the Indigenous cohesion that had been so strong at the start of the 1990s died down toward the end of that decade, partly due to disagreements between local and umbrella organizations regarding representation. By 1998 the Indigenous movement radicalized its actions, occupying oil installations and kidnapping company officials. This switch from peaceful camaraderie to radical action was sparked by frustration among local groups that felt their umbrella organizations failed to defend the rights of those directly affected by oil operations in the field. The era of organized negotiations led by national Indigenous associations had given way to less organized, isolated, and violent actions sponsored by community organizations at the grassroots level. These actions, which were not always supported by umbrella organizations, evidenced division and a struggle for control within the Indigenous movement and ultimately doomed their efforts. The adoption of violent practices incorporated a new level of complexity to the original oil dispute by introducing a new actor, the military, which began to take an active role in imposing oil operations by force.

Fractures or differences of opinion within the Indigenous movement with regard to oil operations are today the rule rather than the exception. One of the most common internal community conflicts concerns community leaders, who represent them in negotiations with companies, governments, and civil organizations. Many times these leaders do not seem to adequately reflect the wishes of the community, or sometimes they are perceived as pursuing their own personal goals instead of those of the majority. Often, leaders are removed by the communities they represent for this reason and are accused of corruption. Some leaders have been accused of living comfortable lives in the capital cities, disconnected from the daily reality of those for whom they are supposed to speak.

Our analysis shows repeated instances of differences among Indigenous federations that represent local communities from a specific area. Where there is a strong presence of international NGOs, it is common for Indigenous federations to compete with one another for funds. Differences among federations make it difficult for oil companies or the government to find credible representative leaders to negotiate with. When this occurs, companies tend to bypass the federations or the Indigenous leaders and adopt the more laborious family-by-family negotiating method, as happened in Peru's Blocks 64 and 101. This less sophisticated negotiating mechanism is very controversial, because it creates conflicts within the community, as some families adopt a favorable position toward the company, while others take the opposite view. Indigenous leaders tend to blame companies for divisions within their organizations or communities. But in truth, it is difficult to measure the extent of cohesion the Indigenous movement had prior to the oil project, and the extent to which divisions came after. What is obvious is that communities unified behind a cause tend to achieve more positive results and experience less conflict than those with a divided front. New conflict stressors are bound to appear when communities lack cohesion or show fractures.

History of Previous Grievances and Noncompliance

Evidence of a previous history of oil grievances or instances when commitments by the parties in a conflict were not honored usually contribute to promoting a united front among Indigenous groups against hydrocarbons development. These two stressors were common to most oil-related conflicts analyzed in this book. Past unresolved or traumatic oil conflicts contribute to building a negative perception of natural resource development. These perceptions in turn set the stage for future disputes when a new oil project materializes. When Indigenous communities are involved, natural resource conflicts may frequently be a consequence of future perceptions. That is, communities may be concerned about the potential threats an oil or gas project may entail rather than with current concrete issues.

In many cases a community may reject a new natural resource project because of memories of past contamination or unfulfilled promises in its territory. Growing communication and solidarity among Indigenous groups throughout the region in the past decades have enabled an exchange of information about past negative externalities linked to oil elsewhere. Indigenous Peoples in Peru know about the seemingly unending legal disputes their counterparts in Ecuador have had with Chevron-Texaco over contamination in the Pastaza province of that country.

This knowledge of past problems, either at home or elsewhere, imprints negative memories and becomes a primary stressor. Communities reject the mere idea of future oil projects in their territory even before they begin or make tougher demands for safeguards and compensation, for fear they may suffer the same fate as others. Sometimes communities may resort to protests or violent actions against a planned oil project as a preventive measure, to avert similar negative environmental or social externalities as in the past. In these cases the perception of future danger, rather than actual dangers, trigger conflicts again. But in these instances that perception is based on empirical data.

Perceptions of threats from an oil or gas project are likely to be influenced by the cultural, historical, or social characteristics of the affected community. A specific tree may have particular healing values for one community; a waterfall may represent evil to another. An Indigenous community will most likely oppose an oil or gas development, even before it starts, if they perceive it could become a threat to the symbolic significance those natural elements have for them.

In Peru the Indigenous group Machiguenga strongly opposed, and eventually blocked, construction of a gas pipeline through the Megantoni National Sanctuary, located in the Cusco department of the province of La Convención in the Echarate district (Martel 2010). The Amazonian sanctuary is symbolically important for the Machiguenga. The best-known area of the sanctuary is the Pongo de Mainiquie (Gorge of the Bears, in the Indigenous Quechua language), a canyon that encompasses various waterfalls that flow into the Urubamba River. The Pongo de Mainiquie represents the origins of their culture and hence has extraordinary significance for them. The magical meaning the Pongo de Mainiquie has for the Machiguengas is magnificently depicted by Peruvian writer Mario Vargas Llosa:

> The bottom of the river in the Gran Pongo is strewn with our corpses. There must be a very great number of them. There they were breathed forth and there they no doubt return to die. That's where they must be, far below the surface, hearing the water moan as it crashes against the stones and dashes against the sharp rocks. That's why there are no turtles above the Pongo, in the mountain reaches. They're good swimmers, but even so, not one of them has ever been able to swim against the current in those waters. The ones that tried drowned. They, too, must be at the bottom now, hearing the shudders

of the world above. That's where we Machiguengas started and that's where we'll end it seems. In the Gran Pongo. (1989, 26)

Once oil work starts in a territory, affected communities experience change: they are confronted with new noises; local rivers carry increased traffic when company boats bring materials and workers in and out; different faces, usually foreigners, walk around the area; and their drinking water from the river sometimes becomes contaminated. Indigenous communities factor in these changes to their lifestyle as costs during compensation negotiations, even before the hydrocarbons project starts in their territory. Nowadays they increasingly include in those costs evidence of historical contamination in locations nearby or in neighboring countries. The closer the community is, either geographically or emotionally, to areas where there is past evidence of oil contamination, the more they will factor in that knowledge in their cost-benefit analyses of potential future oil effects where they live. Indigenous communities will also put a price on possible broken commitments, based on their own experience or on that of Indigenous groups elsewhere.

Many times, unfulfilled agreements or promises lead to conflict or to a delayed resolution of a dispute, as the cases analyzed in this book exemplify. One instance is in relation to the 2006 Dorissa Accords to solve the conflict in Block 1AB, in Peru's northern Amazon province of Loreto. The Dorissa Accords were signed between Pluspetrol, the federal and regional government, the affected Indigenous groups, and the ombudsman. The agreements called for the creation of a multisector commission, with all stakeholders represented, to study, analyze, and propose mechanisms to improve the social and environmental effects of oil operations in the Corrientes River. This initial positive step was later overshadowed by an additional stressor inadvertently brought about by the Dorissa Accords themselves: the lack of compliance to commitments on the part of the regional government. When the government repeatedly failed to comply with its part of the agreements, various protests and violent actions by the Achuar followed, and the intensity of the conflict escalated.

Oil company Pluspetrol complied with its share of the Dorissa Accords: to provide funds for community-development programs and environmental remediation, particularly the reinjection of contaminated waters discharged in the local Corrientes River. But the regional government failed to administer the funds correctly, and the conflict resumed when the Dorissa Accords were not fulfilled.

The Corrientes River area, site of Block 1AB, is not only home to Peru's oldest and most productive oil operation but also the center of the longest exist-ing conflict related to oil on Peruvian soil. As such, Block 1AB has become the main referent for social actions against hydrocarbons development in general throughout the country. Many violent protests against oil operations around the country mirrored the steps followed in Block 1AB, some with high casualties. It was in the Corrientes River that the first contaminated sites were found in the 1990s, the first health problems were detected, the first organized social op-position and violent clashes were reported, and the first attempts to find long-term solutions were made. The main grievances expressed by Indigenous com-munities in this area were related to the health and environmental impacts of oil extraction and the changes to their social and cultural lifestyle. Today, when-ever Indigenous communities oppose oil or gas development in any other part of Peru, the main case in point supporting their opposition or demands is the contamination and life disruption that oil operations brought to their brothers and sisters in the Corrientes River.

BOX 1   A summary of the Corrientes River conflict

The initial contamination of the waters of five regional rivers—Pastaza, Corrientes, Tigres, Samiria, and Amazonas—was reported in 1992 (Gómez García 1995). As with most oil conflicts in Peru, after years of unsuccessful efforts to get government attention to solve grievances, or after failed attempts at dialogue, the strategy adopted by the community was extreme action (Alvarado 2009). Indigenous communities living on the banks of the rivers where Block 1AB is located use the local water to satisfy their basic needs: drinking, cooking, and washing. During the mid-1990s several NGOs reported health problems due to water contamination in the area, but without much response (Servindi 2008). The Ministry of Health started monitoring river contamination in 2001, and in 2007 it published one of the most extensive scientific reports about water contamination in the area (Orta-Martinez et al. 2007). The report found levels of cadmium and lead in the blood of area residents that exceeded by 66.21 percent acceptable levels set by the World Health Organization. By then, Peru's government office in charge of supervising oil and gas investments had already fined oil company Pluspetrol for dumping production water in the rivers.

After learning about the contamination reports, a group of seven hundred Achuar violently took over Block 1AB and interrupted the equivalent of some 50 percent of Peru's total oil production for two weeks. The protests were directed at the failure of the government to abide by an agreement it had signed with members of the Indigenous organization FECONACO in 2004. The agreement included compensation for the oil contamination, along with the design of an economic development plan for their region. The group also brought forward a previous demand for environmental remediation in the Corrientes River.

Perhaps the main legacy of the Corrientes River conflict, which has yet to be fully resolved, is that it established protest as an effective mechanism for obtaining responses to old grievances, particularly in remote areas. Protest actions by the Achuar Indigenous groups of the Corrientes River made history because they led to the unprecedented Dorissa Accords.

Practically all the cases analyzed in this book show a history of lack of compliance with past or present agreements at some point during the development of the conflict. This is true even in the case of comprehensive, well-publicized agreements that involve the participation of the central government and sometimes a well-known mediator, such as the Dorissa Accords in Peru or the Sarayaku Agreements in Ecuador's Block 10. Also within this category are agreements to expand the legal boundaries of the territory of the U'wa Indigenous community in Colombia. Resolution 56 passed by the Instituto Colombiano de la Reforma Agraria on August 6, 1999, increased the U'wa protected area from 151,000 to 220,275 hectares. However, the new borders excluded areas that the U'wa claimed as theirs and that were devoted to oil developments, particularly the site of the Gibraltar field. This led to violent protests in the decades-long conflict.

Noncompliance is particularly high in the hundreds of smaller agreements between companies and communities. The conflict in Block 10 in Ecuador is full of instances of noncompliance by the different parties in the various agreements signed during its long history. In this case, the threat of noncompliance even was used at different times as a bargaining tool during negotiations.

Sometimes, the existence of numerous agreements through the duration of a conflict makes an assessment of overall compliance difficult, if not impossible. There is always bound to be a clause in one accord, or a promise in another, that was not fully fulfilled, and this failure leads to conflict. In many cases, smaller agreements are verbal, which makes it even more difficult to resolve differences, and the dispute then becomes a competition to make the most convincing accusation about the other's failure to meet nonwritten promises. A large backlog of unfulfilled agreements eventually has a cumulative effect on the local population, which feels cheated and may resort to action to express its anger. Our analysis shows that from 2000 to 2010, the arguments used by Indigenous communities for taking action against oil projects increasingly included references to past unfulfilled promises that they either suffered directly or knew about from elsewhere.

THE EXTENT AND NATURE OF CIVIL SOCIETY INVOLVEMENT

We have discussed the evolution of the Indigenous movement in the countries under consideration and how the alliances and interactions among grassroots Indigenous organizations and their umbrella federations may either contribute to conflict resolution or extend disputes. Similarly, as Indigenous activism expands, the nature of the alliances with various national and international NGOs and other organizations has a direct influence on how conflicts develop.

The mapping of civil society in relation to hydrocarbons development in Peru, Ecuador, and Colombia is very complex. Usually, grassroots organizations that represent communities at the local level are affiliated with larger umbrella groups that have a broader, national scope and agenda. Both the local and national organizations may in turn partner with other domestic and international NGOs that provide them with advocacy and technical and financial support. Local Indigenous communities seek partnerships with NGOs to help them present their demands in a structured and educated manner, to disseminate knowledge of their conflict, or to assist as a source of funding. Our analysis identifies several stress elements that can be caused by the complexities of the interrelations among civil society organizations involved in oil conflicts. These elements may get in the way of efforts to resolve hydrocarbons-related disputes.

Difficult Liaisons

Our research found at least three stress elements in relation to the involvement of NGOs in oil conflicts. These stressors sometimes turned efforts at conflict resolution into a more complex enterprise. The first stress element is related to the existence of two opposed positions within the civil society and community-based participation with regard to oil conflicts. One is the total rejection of oil or gas projects; the other is their acceptance, provided civil society is given a green light to lead capacity-building efforts with affected communities to prepare them to negotiate with oil companies. These two types of NGO approaches— combative versus conciliatory, which Fontaine (2007c, 103) characterized as "radical and progressive"—are important in understanding the dynamics of the conflicts, which may develop between two opposed organizations, or between an NGO and local communities or companies.

NGOs that fall within the more radical, combative category are often environmental organizations that reject oil or gas activities due to their negative so-

cial and environmental effects. These more extremist NGOs maintain that Indigenous communities are the best guardians of the Amazon because they are
most interested in preserving it, as its conservation guarantees their own subsistence. They argue that Indigenous Peoples depend on natural resources to
live, which serves to preserve not only the environment but also their collective
identity. This view can explain the alliance between Indigenous and environmental NGOs. Indigenous communities hope their alliance with these NGOs will
help them gain territorial recognition and increased autonomy, which environmental NGOs assume will contribute to preserving the environment.

Within the more conciliatory NGO approach to the oil industry, there usually is no outright rejection of the extractive development, provided it is environmentally and socially sustainable, and it respects the culture and customs of
the communities living in the area. In this approach, NGOs recognize the important economic contribution of extractive industries in general, and oil and
gas in particular, and support the adoption of an environmentally and socially
sustainable agenda for these industries. The expectation among communities
is that NGOs will help them negotiate with oil companies for generating much-
needed jobs and guaranteeing long-deferred basic services.

Radical NGOs usually have a different modus operandi from conciliatory
ones. More combative NGOs transmit their message through actions or cam-
paigns, while conciliatory groups expand their cause through technical assistance to communities. These differences in approaches among NGOs and the
mechanisms they use for expanding their actions converged in Ecuador between the mid-1990s and 2010 in one organization: Frente de Defensa de la
Amazonía (FDA). This group succeeded for the first time in bringing together
Ecuador's environmental, Indigenous, union, and farmers' movements. It provided assistance to both groups: the ones that wanted to negotiate with companies and needed technical support and those that needed guidance on how
to oppose to the oil industry outright (Fontaine 2007c, 104). The most effective
action of this convergence of points of view was seen in 1994 during the campaign known as Amazonía por la Vida, in opposition to Ecuador's Seventh Oil
Bidding Round, which resulted in the licensing of six blocks in the Amazon
jungle. Later, differences within the Frente de Defensa about oil developments
in Yasuni National Park led to its fragmentation.

When the more radical NGOs are involved, conflicts tend to be noisy. These
organizations are rarely community based; rather, they typically pursue a national or sometimes an international agenda. Very often these NGOs, particu-

larly those that have a conservationist agenda and act internationally, are not entirely representative of the viewpoint of local communities, which contributes to tension around their activities (Chapin 2004). Some authors argue that mutual mistrust with local Indigenous organizations is largely born from differences in cultural approaches, priorities, and even timing (Ross 2008, 221).

A second level of stress is linked to the scope of the NGOs involved in the dispute: whether they are national or have international influence. National and international NGOs do not always share goals or agendas. Sometimes an oil conflict may become a tool for a particular NGO to achieve a specific goal that is not necessarily related to the dispute in question. For example, a local NGO may use the conflict to acquire national or political notoriety or to gain a position abroad that may eventually open doors to international organizations or to donors. International NGOs are instrumental in attracting overseas attention to local conflicts around oil and gas developments that would otherwise go unnoticed. In Peru much of the international attention around the Camisea natural gas project came from the actions of international NGOs, which were active in scrutinizing the project from the start. The Nature Conservancy, the World Wildlife Fund for Nature, the Smithsonian Institution, and Conservation International joined Peruvian civil society during the early stages of Camisea to voice their concerns in a letter to the financing institutions of the Inter-American Development Bank and U.S. EximBank (Conservation International 2006). This gave the Camisea conflict international and national visibility from early on. By contrast, oil contamination in Peru's northern Amazon jungle (Block 1AB-8) was made public initially by Peruvian NGOs and Indigenous federations. But these organizations lacked the muscle to expand the case both at home and abroad. It was not until many years later, when international NGOs became involved, that the Corrientes River conflict acquired national and international attention.

It is difficult to conclude whether the internationalization of a conflict contributes to solving it. The examples of Camisea in Peru, Sarayaku (Block 10) in Ecuador, and the U'wa (Block Samore) in Colombia show that early mobilization of vocal international NGOs creates incentives for governments and companies to internalize the negative externalities and attend to the grievances and demands of local communities. Furthermore, several case studies demonstrate that the contribution of civil society to ensure early involvement of the affected population—such as through the monitoring of oil activities for assessing the degree and type of effect they have on communities' lives—may prove to be an effective conflict mitigation tool down the line. Scholars have warned, however, against building too many expectations of civil society, which is required to monitor government and company compliance alike and also to set checks on the discretionary power of elites (Carbonnier, Brugger, and Krause 2011, 247–64).

Finally, a third element adding stress to the role of NGOs in oil-related conflicts is the difficulty in finding truly representative voices among Indigenous organizations. This constitutes a major risk for NGOs, particularly the large international ones, who put much of their reputation at times in the hands of those local leaders. As mentioned earlier, Indigenous groups are often divided or suspicious of one another when confronted with oil projects. Within one region there may be a variety of points of view with regard to a particular development or to extractive industries in general. Even within one community, there are contradictory and evolving views on whether to welcome the oil project or not and on the compensation to demand in exchange. These divisions are reflected in the political or national alliances communities make, as is the case with the two grassroots federations that represent communities from the Corrientes River: Federación de Pueblos Indígenas del Bajo y Alto Corrientes (FEPIBAC) and Federación de Comunidades Nativas del Río Corrientes (FECONACO). Each of these federations is affiliated with one of two conflicting national organizations: the more conciliatory Confederación de Nacionalidades de la Amazonía Peruana (CONAP) and the combative Asociación Interétnica de Desarrollo de la Selva Peruana (AIDESEP). The inability of Indigenous groups to come to an agreement on a single local or national representative voice was a major stumbling block in solving the Corrientes River conflict throughout the history of the dispute.

Community differences may be exacerbated by the presence of NGOs with diverse agendas, which in turn contributes to aggravating the conflict. In Ecuador's Block 24 the Sarayaku Indigenous group maintained a relatively homogenous opposition to oil developments in their territories for decades, but they were sometimes also confronted with detractors within the group. In 1999 Indigenous community members from Taisha, in the province of Morona-Santiago, attempted to reach agreements with the oil company, but they were soon reprimanded by the majority population that had been apparently rallied by radical NGOs to reject extractive activities altogether. These new divisions among local communities added a new layer to the conflict that needed to be resolved first, before tackling the underlying dispute related to the presence of oil operations in their territory.

This confusing landscape of divided communities and NGOs with different agendas makes it difficult to develop a structured and well-coordinated civil society strategy that adequately represents the interests of affected communities. Our case studies in the three countries show that the lack of a united front, not only among local communities but also within civil society, exacerbates oil-related conflicts. Companies, and sometimes governments, use these different views and disagreements among Indigenous organizations and NGOs to their own advantage, by trying to tilt the balance one way or the other.

Consultation and Participation: One Voice

For all the differences that prevent Indigenous communities and civil society organizations from coming together with a unified voice with respect to hydrocarbons developments, there is one topic they all agree on and they all invariably raise: the need to consult with local communities prior to an oil development. This is one of the most controversial issues and a major stress element in most oil-related conflicts in Latin America.

The right of Indigenous Peoples to be consulted is stated in the ILO Convention 169 that Peru signed in 1993, Colombia in 1991, and Ecuador in 1998, and by the UN Declaration on the Rights of Indigenous Peoples, of which the three countries are also signatories.[4] Each country has developed the concept of consultation further through various legal instruments and institutional initiatives.[5] Ecuador went as far as to include the concept of free prior informed consultation with Indigenous communities in article 57 of its National Constitution. In 2008 Colombia created, through Resolution 3598, a special working group within the Ministry of the Interior and Justice to oversee the implementation of prior consultation with Indigenous and Afro-Colombian groups in various projects. Also, the country's Constitutional Tribunal ratified the right to consultation in several rulings throughout the years and declared itself opposed to legislation that fails to respect it. Peru's Congress approved the Law of Previous Consultation in 2011, after a tedious consensus-building process, as stated in chapter 3.

However, in spite of these efforts, the matter of consultation in oil and gas projects continues to be controversial and the source of many conflicts. The quality and extent of the process is the subject of vehement conflict in the three countries under study in this book. All three countries implement some kind of consultation, but it is usually deemed incomplete by Indigenous Peoples and the civil society that supports them. In Ecuador a national debate on the mechanism of prior consultation when applied to water (Univision.com 2010) and mining (*El Tiempo* 2010) laws resulted in violent clashes in 2010. That year, the Law of Citizen Participation passed by Congress did not meet the expectations of civil society because it failed to make the process of free prior and informed consent legally binding (*Diario Hoy* 2010b). In Colombia there are many complaints that in spite of the existence of several legal instruments that call for prior consultation, in practice local Indigenous communities are consulted after an oil contract has already been signed.

The main sources of contention are differences in the interpretation of *consultation*. For Indigenous communities, consulting gives them the right to decide if an extractive project may or may not be implemented in their territory. However, the ILO Convention 169 that defines the mechanisms for consultation falls short of granting communities veto power over an extractive project. The legally binding convention encourages consent from Indigenous Peoples as a guiding principle throughout the document but does not stipulate the obligation to obtain it as a prerequisite for implementing a particular project in their territories. The UN Declaration on the Rights of Indigenous Peoples, by contrast, not only stresses the need for states to consult with Indigenous communities on issues that affect them but also emphasizes in various parts of the document that getting free, prior, and informed consent should be a requisite in certain matters.[6] But the declaration is not binding.

Perhaps the fuzzy wording of article 6.1(a) in ILO Convention 169, which calls for the consultation process to be carried out "through appropriate procedures," is what makes its implementation difficult, confusing, and less than satisfying for Indigenous Peoples. The vague wording likely reflects the long-term controversy around this issue, which became apparent during the process of debating the convention. Governments gradually increased their awareness and modified their approach toward Indigenous issues, although with limitations when it came to granting self-government and territorial rights.

In addition to the controversies created by the process of consultation, communities and NGOs often complain about poor participatory mechanisms. In practice, participatory activities and community-relations programs, including the process of consultation, are usually organized around the Environmental Impact Assessment (EIA), the ultimate document that guarantees a project will be environmentally and socially sound. The laws of the three countries require EIAS of oil and gas projects.[7]

The EIA has been much criticized in the three countries. Communities claim it does not truly represent their points of view and that it is biased because the responsibility for preparing the document usually rests on the company itself, which is an interested party (Gil 2009). A major grudge among communities is that they are often consulted for the first time about a particular hydrocarbons project only when the EIA is being prepared, which is after the oil or gas license has been granted.

An analysis of how the participatory mechanisms and the consultation process is implemented in Peru for the development of oil and gas projects serves to show how complex and difficult this issue can become. Of a total of 288 social conflicts reported by the Office of the Ombudsman in September 2009, 44 percent—or 126—were related to problems with the consultation process (Fundación 2010, 46). In the case of hydrocarbons activities, there are specific legal steps that need to be followed to ensure citizen participation.[8] There are an initial participatory event (Evento Presencial) and three subsequent workshops facilitated by the Ministry of Energy and Mines and organized during the design of the EIA. These events become an exchange of information by which the local population learns from the government about plans to give out oil or gas licenses in their territory, and at the same time the local population communicates their fears and doubts.

For the government, these four participatory events fulfill the requirements of the citizen participation regulations and of the prior consultation demanded by international law (essentially the ILO 169 Convention) in the case of Indigenous communities.[9] Local communities and the civil society, however, have a different take. They see the process as not participatory enough and argue that it merely informs them of an oil project that will be developed in their territories without giving them the option to veto it, because in most cases the license has already been granted before these workshops take place. It is common to hear from community members that by the time the company and the central government ask them what they think of the project, it is too late because the license has already been given to the company.

The circumstances that led to the bloody events in Peru's northwestern Amazon province of Bagua in 2009 provide a good case study for analyzing the main factors that contribute to conflicts around the issue of consultation. After two months of protests by Indigenous Peoples, deadly clashes with the police resulted in dozens of dead and wounded. The motivation for the Bagua protests was a series of new presidential decrees the Indigenous population believed infringed on their rights.

The protests followed an Amazonian strike by Indigenous communities from throughout the Peruvian Amazon that unified to oppose the government decrees (Servindi 2009a). The protesters had two demands: amendments to the constitution to restore territorial rights they had lost in 1993 and the proper use of free, prior, and informed consent, as expressed by the ILO Convention 169. For them, this consent meant the ability to accept or reject an oil project in their territory, although the ILO Convention 169 does not specifically grant this right.

The bloodshed of the Bagua events served to open up a national debate about the consultation process that ended in an initial consultation bill passed in May 2010. Designed after months of negotiations between opposed parties, with the mediation of the ombudsman, the bill called for mandatory consultation with communities about development projects that affect them (Lizarzaburu 2010). But the bill was revised by President Alan García, who argued that if no consensus was reached during the consultation process, the state—and not local Indigenous communities—would have the final word. This move effectively took away from Indigenous communities the power to veto hydrocarbons projects in their territories. The Law of Previous Consultation was finally approved by Congress in 2011 but is still widely opposed by Indigenous groups.

Continued opposition to the Law of Previous Consultation will most likely impede its successful application; for the law to be effective it needs approval by popular consensus lest it be voided by the same imperfections it is trying to correct. The debate on the law placed Peru in a tight spot: opposition to the law could lead to outright opposition to extractive industries in general in the future, which could in turn jeopardize the country's economic growth potential.

This example shows the tensions that prevail around this issue, mainly born from different opinions on the extent of the consultation process. In short, there are extreme and opposing views of the meaning of consultation, and legal interpretations that could help to shed some light on the controversy are often vague. In the view of Indigenous communities and civil society, the process of consultation should introduce the notion of free and prior informed consent. By this they understand that the following three conditions should be met: consultations should take place prior to the signing of an oil contract, or before even considering signing one; the Indigenous communities should be provided with all the details of the project in a timely manner; and, most important, communities should have a right to veto the project. This position has been greatly championed by the UN Permanent Forum on Indigenous Issues but highly contested by governments.

In some cases, governments see a consultation law that grants the power of veto to a minority group as detrimental to the country's sovereignty. According to this view, such a law would be a major breach of the nation-state principle, which maintains that the wealth and natural resources of a country should benefit all citizens and thus cannot be claimed by a minority group within the population. This argument was expressed in the observations to the consultation law that the government of Peru presented in 2010:

> It is necessary for the bill to explicitly establish that the result of the consultation process does not limit, suspend or prohibit the State from adopting decisions aimed at protecting and guaranteeing the general interest of the Nation, which should be on top of any other interest. This is in view of the fact that the [ILO] Convention 169 does not grant Indigenous Populations any privilege over other members of the Nation. (Government Observations 2010)

Tensions and controversy about the nature and quality of the consultation process exist in practically every case study analyzed in this book. Our analysis shows that taking minor steps to improve the consultation mechanism, such as reinforcing transparency and participation before the start of the hydrocarbons project, can go a long way in mitigating the risk of conflicts down the line. This is true even when governments do not recognize communities' power of veto. But a permanent solution to the controversy surrounding consultation in relation to oil projects will most likely not happen any time soon in Latin America, because regardless of whether the local community may or may not have veto power over a project, as explained in chapter 3, it is the state that holds the ultimate constitutional prerogative on when, how, and if to develop subsoil resources.

AVAILABILITY AND EFFICIENCY OF INSTITUTIONAL MEDIATION

Well-designed and effectively applied mediation by the central government is key to reducing conflicts. When a conflict arises between an Indigenous community and a company, both sides normally try to find solutions between themselves first, without involving third parties. If these efforts fail, the community often demands the intervention of the government. In fact, even when the bilateral negotiations do end up in an agreement, Indigenous communities many times demand some kind of government validation, as a way of guaranteeing that the parties will commit to their promises. If there is no such government response, the process is usually seen as lacking institutional grounding, and the risk of open conflict is intensified. In most cases of successful resolution, the institutionalization of the conflict contributes to reducing its intensity, at least for some time, while the actors involved negotiate or reframe their demands and actions.

The Negative Example of Ecuador's Block 10

The long history of conflict in Ecuador's Block 10 illustrates how the absence of a solid and well-thought-out central government mediation strategy during the initial phases of the project resulted in the loss of trust in the authorities and in more conflict. Block 10 spreads over a roughly five-hundred-thousand-acre zone inhabited by seventeen Indigenous communities. State presence in the area has been historically minimal, which created an institutional vacuum that was partially filled by the oil operators (Torres Dávila 2005, 31–38). Disputes in Block 10 continued for more than two decades and went through various stages of confrontation, negotiation, agreements, and disagreements, but with little solid government involvement.

The initial phase of the conflict in Block 10—between 1992 and 1998—was marked by an important mobilization of the Indigenous movement. During this first part of the conflict, blanket opposition to oil developments in the area by OPIP resulted in direct clashes with oil company ARCO. An alliance between local Indigenous organizations and international NGOs that acted as mediators led to the signing of agreements in Plano, Texas, to reduce tensions. The agreements involved all the main stakeholders: the oil company, local organizations, and the government. But the initial equilibrium eventually failed because the agreements were never implemented, and conflict erupted again. The involvement of the government in this phase of the conflict was limited to being a mere signatory to the Plano Agreements.

The second phase of the conflict—1998–2002—was marked by the departure of ARCO, whose operations were taken over in 2000 by its partner in the consortium, AGIP, amid a serious political and economic crisis in the country. At this time, the conflict was marked by a series of individual agreements between AGIP and the communities directly affected by its oil operations, with little government participation. There started to be divisions among Indigenous organizations and between the communities they represented. These divisions, in turn, generated an overall uneasiness that was further exacerbated by AGIP's failure to assume its share of responsibility for the effect of its activities in the area. In 2002 the Indigenous federations presented an integral regional development plan that was to be funded by AGIP at one million U.S. dollars per year (Torres Dávila 2005, 31–38).

But by 2005 AGIP's failure to shoulder its financial commitments marked the third phase of the conflict — 2005–9. At that point, the umbrella Indigenous organization Asociación de Desarrollo Indígena Región Amazonica (ASODIRA) called for the intervention of the Ministry of Energy and Mines (MEM). The ministry failed to respond, and so the Indigenous groups took action. They first banned flights that brought AGIP contractors to the oil site and threatened to seize the oil wells. They called for a strike, receiving the support of Indigenous federations from several provinces. In Pastaza enraged Indigenous groups took over AGIP oil installations and burned a company building. The military intervened, and there were reports of fifty-six persons injured, both civilians and military personnel.

Block 10 illustrates the failure to mitigate the conflict primarily due to lack of solid institutional mediation. A tense political situation in Ecuador also had a major impact and certainly contributed to the failure to implement the Plano Agreements during the first phase of the conflict. In the second half of the third phase of the conflict, the intervention of representatives from the National Congress and local government mediators was key to mitigating the disputes.

Graph 11 shows the upward tendency in conflict intensity in Block 10, as attempts by Indigenous communities to engage the government failed between 2005 and 2006. By contrast, graph 12 shows the reverse trend, as conflict intensity diminished following the signing of a financial agreement between the umbrella Indigenous organization ASODIRA and the company in February 2007 (Galvez 2007). The agreement had the active involvement of representatives from the National Congress Committee on Amazonian Issues, and local government representatives acted as mediators (*El Comercio.com* 2007).

The Positive Example of the Peruvian Ombudsman

A positive example of government intervention in socioenvironmental conflicts is in Peru, particularly the role that the Office of the Ombudsman has been

GRAPH 11   Conflict intensity increases

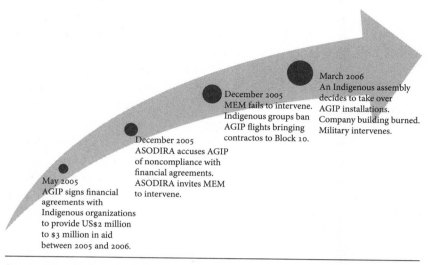

March 2006
An Indigenous assembly
decides to take over
AGIP installations.
Company building burned.
Military intervenes.

December 2005
MEM fails to intervene.
Indigenous groups ban
AGIP flights bringing
contractos to Block 10.

December 2005
ASODIRA accuses AGIP
of noncompliance with
financial agreements.
ASODIRA invites MEM
to intervene.

May 2005
AGIP signs financial
agreements with
Indigenous organizations
to provide US$2 million
to $3 million in aid
between 2005 and 2006.

Source: Compiled by the author with data from *El Comercio.com* (2005a, 2005b, 2005c, 2006, 2007a) and Fontaine (2004, 2009).

GRAPH 12   Conflict intensity decreases

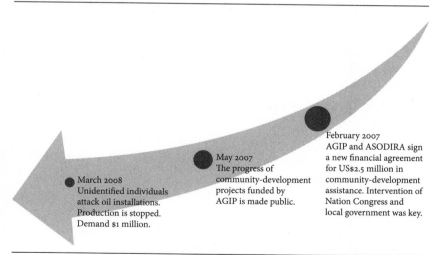

February 2007
AGIP and ASODIRA sign
a new financial agreement
for US$2.5 million in
community-development
assistance. Intervention of
Nation Congress and
local government was key.

May 2007
The progress of
community-development
projects funded by
AGIP is made public.

March 2008
Unidentified individuals
attack oil installations.
Production is stopped.
Demand $1 million.

Source: Compiled by the author with data from *El Comercio.com* (2007b, 2008).

playing in solving these disputes. The Peruvian ombudsman has become the only figure capable of effective conflict prevention and management, in a way that brings opposed parties to some kind of understanding and agreement. Unlike Colombia and Ecuador, where the Office of the Ombudsman typically lacks the moral recognition needed for that institution to fulfill its mandate properly, in Peru the institution has grown in stature and popular respect ever since its creation in 1996. The intervention of the Peruvian ombudsman does not necessarily solve conflicts; however, its presence has been key in helping to reduce the intensity of disputes and in opening avenues for dialogue.

Since its creation, the Peruvian Office of the Ombudsman has enjoyed an exceptionally high level of public approval and a unique degree of legitimacy among government organizations in Latin America. The role of the ombudsman is to protect the constitutional and fundamental rights of persons and communities, to supervise state acts and responsibilities, and to make sure public services are provided. The office is an autonomous organization with a mandate given by articles 161 and 162 of the 1993 National Constitution and an operating structure defined by its Organic Law (no. 26520), passed on August 8, 1995.

The Peruvian ombudsman has from the outset gone beyond its constitutional mandate when addressing some of the issues that are the underlying causes of conflict in relation to oil and gas developments.[10] As part of its task, the office gives particular emphasis to addressing some of Peru's most pressing social fractures, aiming at excluding racism and all forms of discrimination (Office of the Ombudsman 2009a, 5). These social fractures are usually at the center of energy conflicts common in areas inhabited by poor populations or by Indigenous Peoples who have lived through decades of economic, political, and social marginalization and a chronic lack of basic services.

Although mediation is not specifically listed in its constitutional mandate, the description of the ombudsman's tasks is broad enough to allow it to take the role of mediator in conflicts (Pegram 2008, 57). Of the total 347 social conflicts in which the Ombudsman Office intervened during 2009, almost half were social or environmental in nature—that is, related to the control of, use of, or access to natural resources (Office of the Ombudsman 2009a, 247). Some complaints were presented by Indigenous communities that claimed not to have been consulted prior to the arrival of an oil exploration project in their territory. A few complaints denounced plans for developing oil in one reserved zone, Güeppi, and two soon-to-be-reserved areas—Napo Tigre and Napo Curaray in the Department of Loreto.[11] Other hydrocarbons complaints received by the ombudsman that year included one related to gas leaks, from a community living close to a natural gas plant.[12] There were others related to fear of future environmental contamination from planned oil exploration activities.

The structure of the Office of the Ombudsman makes it more agile and able to intervene in such cases than the regular judicial channels. It has offices dispersed around the country and a system of mobile units that travel to remote regions where there is little or no institutional presence (Office of the Ombudsman 2009a). Citizens may present claims for free, or may even transmit them verbally, which makes the whole process very approachable, requiring no prior knowledge of how the judicial system works. For affected Indigenous communities living in remote areas, knowing there is an ombudsman station close to them where they can easily express their complaints without needing prior legal assistance acts as an incentive for bringing in their cases. The ombudsman may present cases directly to the highest court of the country, the Constitutional Court, or to the Inter-American Human Rights Tribunal with no need to go through domestic legal procedures, which may be long and convoluted and sometimes corrupt. This ease of action gives the ombudsman considerable power.

The Office of the Ombudsman enjoys a high degree of legitimacy among the population, especially within the most vulnerable groups, thanks in part to this ease of access to the institution. Most likely it began to build that popular trust after its supervisory work and subsequent open criticism of procedural flaws during the run-up to the controversial 2000 presidential elections (Office of the Ombudsman 2002). At that time, the office stood in contrast to the generalized corruption and semiauthoritarianism that characterized the last term of President Alberto Fujimori. An opinion poll in 2010 gave the office the highest rating—53 percent—among government institutions considered to be most trustworthy for fighting corruption. This confidence in the ombudsman exists in a country where people see corruption as the number one problem to be resolved, according to the same poll (Transparency International 2010b).

The role of the ombudsman in mitigating energy conflicts has been pivotal. In half of the hydrocarbons conflicts studied in Peru during our investigation, the intervention of the ombudsman was instrumental in diffusing disputes. The actions taken by the ombudsman varied according to the nature of each conflict, but in general they can be grouped in three categories: those aimed at forging dialogue between the actors, preventive actions prior to the actual

TABLE 5   Intervention of the ombudsman in Peru

Conflict	Description of ombudsman action	Type of intervention
Block 1AB/8	Mediates in negotiations that lead to the signing of the Dorissa Accords. Monitors Dorissa compliance. (October 2006)	Mediation
Block 39	Participates in Multisector Commission for Communities in Isolation to protect peoples in voluntary isolation who may be affected by hydrocarbons projects. (March 2009)	Preventive action
Block 64	Promotes dialogue between the affected communities and oil company Talisman. (January 2009)	Dialogue
Block 107	Warns that hydrocarbons activities could damage uncontacted groups. (January 2006)	Preventive action
Block 117	Declares need to establish dialogue. (October 2009)	Dialogue
Blocks 135 and 137	Facilitates dialogue between the oil company, the Matses Indigenous community, and the local and national government. (February 2009)	Dialogue
Block 155	Makes conflict public. (2009)	Preventive action
Blocks Z-1, 22, and 23 (offshore)	Mediates in negotiations with all parties. (November 2009)	Mediation

Source: Compiled by the author with data from the Office of the Ombudsman of Peru (2011).

development of a conflict, and mediation in active conflicts to reduce their intensity. Table 5 summarizes the role of the Peruvian ombudsman in some of the case studies analyzed.

In all cases, the presence of the ombudsman was key to mitigating the intensity of the conflict by opening alternative options to violence. However, it is clear that the ombudsman does not independently resolve conflicts. Rather, it succeeds in bringing the parties together to a negotiating table, which in turn may reduce the intensity of the dispute by creating a negotiating space. Its mediating action may even fail at times, but in the end it is the only entity that seems to possess the necessary power to convene the parties and help them to reconsider their actions. In the case of Blocks Z-1, 22, and 23, for example, the initial mediation of the ombudsman on November 11 led to dialogue. However, the dialogue broke six days later in spite of the participation of the ombudsman, leading to a protest and the blocking of the north Pan-American highway for several days. The opposed parties were finally brought back to the negotiating table three days later; this time the ombudsman and the regional government acted as mediators.

The main tool at the Peruvian ombudsman's disposal for successful intervention in hydrocarbons conflicts is probably its high esteem among all actors in the conflict, which contributes to making the ombudsman's voice heard during the usually confusing initial dispute period. Unlike a government prosecutor, the ombudsman lacks coercive authority. Instead, it emits nonbinding resolutions and reports based on citizens' complaints. It relies on the media to disseminate its findings through daily, weekly, and monthly reports of conflicts. It also has important allies, such as local NGOs, international donors, and the church, to ensure its message is delivered and to guarantee independence from the government. This support from different sectors of society ensures the integrity of the Office of the Ombudsman in case of political attacks (Pegram 2008, 66).

Two other key elements that contribute to the high regard of the Office of the Ombudsman in Peru are its total independence to perform its tasks and the fact that it enjoys similar immunity from prosecution, as do members of Congress. This immunity, its unrestricted powers of investigation, and the obligation of public bodies to cooperate put the institution in a powerful position to research issues, convince opposed parties to pursue a dialogue, and even in some cases to provide new impetus for negotiations. Normally, by the time the ombudsman is called on to intervene, the conflict has escalated to critical levels, as when dialogue has been suspended between contending parties or when there are violent protests or the seizing of oil infrastructure.

In Peru the cases we analyzed showed a distinctive pattern of conflict escalation, then subsequent decline when the ombudsman was summoned to intervene. Our case studies, and the Peruvian experience more generally, show that effective and timely mediation can be key for reducing conflicts and for leading opposed parties to negotiation. Interestingly, even where government actions are often ineffective in mediating conflicts, communities tend to demand the intervention of the state when conflicts reach unmanageable levels. This is not necessarily because they trust a specific ministry or government, but because they perceive that conflict mediation is a fundamental and legitimate role the government should play. The case of the ombudsman of Peru shows how independent state structures that hold a high degree of legitimacy can be instrumental in reducing tensions and bringing stakeholders to negotiate.

STRATEGIES FOR THE ADOPTION OF
SAFEGUARDS AND SERVICE DELIVERY

Over the past decade large oil companies have become more conscious of negative effects on their general image and among stakeholders when they do not pursue sound social and environmental policies in the countries where they operate. For that reason, they have increasingly engaged in voluntary schemes, such as Corporate Social Responsibility, the United Nations Global Compact, and the World Bank Extractive Industry Transparency Initiative, as a guarantee of their high social and environmental standards. Their performance abroad is increasingly being scrutinized by regulators in their countries of origin as a way of monitoring their social and environmental behavior. This socially and environmentally conscious modus operandi is built around international efforts to mitigate the negative externalities of the oil industry, including environmental pollution, social disruptions, corruption, and mismanagement of oil revenues.

Within this context, most large oil corporations (known as "majors" in the industry) now have special departments with trained professionals devoted to ensuring the implementation of Corporate Social Responsibility.[13] Throughout the years this notion has been expanded from its original focus on workers' rights and the environment. Today, it includes the need to ensure transparent corporate accounting methods and the understanding that business can be a tool for reducing poverty and ensuring sustainable economic growth in the developing world.

Still, there is a great deal of controversy around the potential for Corporate Social Responsibility to effectively meet its rather ambitious goal of making significant social, environmental, and economic contributions to the countries where large corporations operate. Back in the 1970s Nobel Laureate economist Milton Friedman rejected the idea of having businesses involved in social welfare for fear it would distract them from their main goal of maximizing profits for shareholders (Friedman 1970). This view was challenged as shareholders and activists in the developed world became increasingly aware of the environmental and social impacts of large corporations around the world. Large European and American oil multinationals, and a growing number of middle-sized

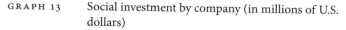

GRAPH 13   Social investment by company (in millions of U.S. dollars)

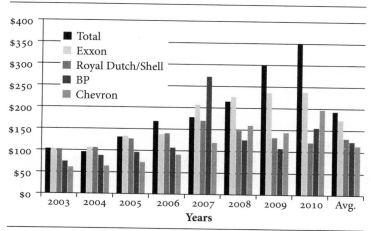

Source: Compiled by author from company data (Total 2011; Total Foundation 2010; ExxonMobil 2003–11; BP 2003–11; Royal Dutch Shell 2003–10; Chevron 2003–11).

Data for ConocoPhillips is incomplete and for that reason is not included in the graph.

businesses, are willing to spend increasing amounts of capital to improve the economic well-being of the local communities in the areas where they operate. These companies are increasingly committed to adopting more stringent social and environmental standards abroad, in response to demands from shareholders and NGOs at home. Graph 13 shows the upward tendency of social investment by the largest world oil-producing companies from an average total of $450 million in 2003 to $1 billion in 2010.

One of the main complaints put forth by Indigenous communities living in oil areas is the lack of government presence, particularly the central government, especially in relation to service delivery, the provision of justice, and sometimes even security. The void left by the state in these areas is often filled by oil companies. The downside of giving companies a more prominent role in alleviating poverty is that it may conceal a very serious underlying problem: the weakness, or sometimes the lack of political will, on the part of host governments to take that role by implementing a national agenda that supports effective social inclusion, particularly in remote oil areas.

In their role as providers of basic needs, companies make short-term decisions: to build a much-needed school or a hospital, for example. This modus operandi, with the private company taking center stage in the provision of social welfare, indicates a fundamental flaw: the absence of well-planned social development policies designed with the participation of local communities. With no such policies in place to use as guidance, the generalized perception is that the authorities apply quick one-time solutions to local grievances, and companies impose their own community programs. Tensions in this situation build around a general feeling of mistrust among the communities that briefly become the center of government and corporate attention but that have been historically forgotten by the state and society as a whole.

Historically, the most common recipient of the grievances of these isolated communities has been the church, followed by NGOs working in the area. When oil companies suddenly take center stage, then, communities react defensively, knowing that had it not been for interest in oil or gas reserves in their territory, they would still be unnoticed by the authorities and the world in general. They wonder if the companies are really interested in improving their living conditions, or if they just want to extract revenues from the hydrocarbons reserves in their territories, regardless of any benefits for the communities. These concerns denote a high degree of uncertainty and much skepticism. These feelings may be further emphasized by information circulated by NGOs and church organizations about cases elsewhere of oil developments that failed to improve the economic and social conditions of the local population.

Social Support in the Hands of Oil Companies

Companies engage in a process of quasi-continual negotiations with the local Indigenous communities affected by an oil project. These exchanges are aimed at establishing the right of way for the company to access the oil or gas reserves it wants to develop in the Indigenous lands. The price the company pays to access the oil and gas is often in the form of the provision of basic needs and services, such as drinking water, a hospital, a school, or transportation in and out of remote areas. The government typically becomes a mere observer, or at best a facilitator of the negotiations, in what locals often see as a relinquishment of its responsibilities.

The advantages obtained from negotiations with companies are often the most tangible benefits local communities obtain from the oil project. This is particularly true when structural flaws of the kind discussed in chapter 3 prevent oil revenues from flowing from the central government to the provincial or local coffers or when the funds are not invested for the benefit of the local population. Given the absence of sound government-sponsored local development programs and the limited state presence in the remote areas where oil and gas projects are developed, social and investment decisions for local communities usually result primarily from these bilateral negotiations between companies and community leaders.

Defining the local development agenda through bilateral negotiations becomes a function of the power relations between the company and the local groups. The company's strategy is to convince the local population to agree to its oil project. This, they argue, is important to ensure minimal costly disturbances throughout the life of the project, although in practice there is no clear-cut guarantee. For the communities these negotiations are usually the only opportunity they have for improving their living standards, through obtaining from companies access to the basic needs they lack. Often, there is not just one agreement with the company, but several, signed with a variety of communities at different times during the oil or gas project. Each agreement responds to different community needs, aspirations, and positions on economic development. Sometimes negotiations within one community vary from family to family, so the company may make individual agreements with each. Often, the agreements are verbal.

A development plan designed this way, in response to the needs of each microsituation, usually lacks a coherent overall goal for the region and for the population as a whole, resulting in a circular pattern by which conflicts grow as the number of new microagreements increase. This is what happened in Ecuador's Block 10, where failed attempts at adopting a comprehensive development plan led to this kind of micromanagement style after the Sarayaku Agreements were signed in 1989. One of the main achievements of the Sarayaku Agreements had been the passage of a series of national laws regarding hydrocarbons activities, including rules for environmental and social remediation, for example, that were expected to ultimately benefit local Indigenous communities living close to the oil projects. But without previously identified local development priorities and an integral plan to put them in practice, implementation of the new laws was weak at the local level, and communities failed to see much improvement to their livelihood. It was to make up for that legal sluggishness that the communities engaged in individual negotiations with the oil company to obtain direct solutions to their grievances. This set the stage for the micromanagement style that ensued, which resulted in three separate community agreements between the company and local communities signed in 1991: two for providing general assistance to the Moretecocha, Pandanuque, and Santa Cecilia communities (Fontaine 2004; Crespo Plaza 2007, 207–27) and, third, a labor agreement to help community members from Santa Cecilia and Moretecocha.

The process of signing individual agreements in Block 10 resulted in three levels of conflict: among families of the same community, between communities and their umbrella organizations, and among communities in the same area. In the first case, the multiplicity of microaccords among various families belonging to a specific community created competition among them for obtaining more from the company. Second, arrangements between particular communities or families and the company left the umbrella Indigenous organization out, which created friction. Third, communities came into conflict with regard to their stance on the oil project or potential benefits from it, such as jobs. This was further exacerbated by the tendency among oil companies to give higher benefits to those living closer to the project, generating one of the most common sources of tension among communities.

In the medium to long term, the lack of permanent answers to people's problems resulted in renewed grievances, more one-on-one company-community solutions, and more conflict. A circular pattern has thus been established by which a microagreement is reached, creating conflicts when communities are not happy with the results or when they demand more, which in turn leads to another microagreement that results in another layer of conflicts, and so on.

One-on-one development agreements between companies and communities, without an overall development plan, have obvious negative consequences: they build dependence on the company and they contribute to creating perverse competition and eventually conflict among the actors supposed to benefit from the accords. Dependence on the company presents several downsides. For example, it breeds a permanent state of dissatisfaction that in turn fuels latent conflict when communities feel increasingly dependent. It also fosters paternalistic attitudes and raises questions about the future sustainability and quality of the services once the oil or gas license ends. This concern is being addressed in a few exceptional cases, such as Ecuador's Block 16, where Spanish oil company Repsol has a contract until 2018 and devotes one million U.S. dollars per year in compensation and training programs for the local Waorani Indigenous community. The company was considering the creation of a trust fund that would continue to finance part of those expenses once its license ends.[14] But in general, these postlicense sustainability mechanisms are still rare.

High oil prices make investing in high-risk environmentally and socially sensitive areas, such as the Amazon, more cost effective for companies. Fewer available conventional oil reserves elsewhere turn these areas into valuable options, so companies are willing to go further in their negotiations with communities to access the reserves in their territories. Local communities try to use this yearning for their territories to their advantage, by increasing their demands or by threatening to take action if demands are not met. In the end, the quality, quantity, and sophistication of the development projects are defined by the market value of the oil areas rather than by local needs, because it represents how much the company is willing to give in exchange for accessing the oil sites.

When large multinational companies take the lead in providing services in an area, the historical absence and inefficiency of the state is underscored. How this cycle of events affects concerned Indigenous communities' feelings of citizenship and belonging to the broader nation remains unclear. Certainly the lack of government involvement for overseeing the design and long-term sustainability of a development plan that responds to the needs of the community does not help the situation. Ultimately, having companies as the sole interlocutors of communities in relation to the development of local services does not reduce tensions and conflicts. If anything, our case studies show that it contributes to generating more conflictive situations.

The piecemeal approach to local development is one reason many conflicts do not disappear and remain latent. The situation becomes more complex with increases in the number of oil projects that exist, the amount of social funding involved, and the differences in the quality of social development provided by the various companies. In the long run, the main concern is whether a piecemeal approach can generate sustainable long-term answers to social issues, without generating stubborn conflicts that lead to negative dynamics among the stakeholders involved.

Different Approaches to Safeguards: Majors versus Juniors

It would be wrong to judge the social and environmental performance of all oil companies in the same way, because each oil corporation has its own unique operating style. Companies differ greatly in the way they incorporate environmental and social safeguards and on the degree of significance they grant to these. In negotiations with local communities, large oil companies normally devote large teams of professionals that are part of specially created community-relations departments. Their relatively comfortable financial situation allows large corporations to be much more generous in their programs to compensate affected communities and more thorough when it comes to monitoring the social and environmental impacts of their operations.

By contrast, smaller, or "junior," oil companies normally lack the financial muscle of their larger partners for investing in efficient Corporate Social Responsibility policies. Perhaps most important, oil juniors, which are sometimes privately owned, are generally less concerned about their image, because they do not have to respond to shareholder scrutiny. In the same vein, national oil companies are typically governed by social and environmental rules of their country of origin that may not be the most rigorous in the market. Chinese national oil companies, which are increasingly making their way into Latin America, have built a reputation of being rather lax when it comes to incorporating the latest internationally acceptable social, environmental, and labor standards (Shankleman 2009).

To better grasp the differences between majors and juniors it is important to understand how the oil industry works. Juniors tend to be primarily focused on the initial exploration phase of oil projects before actual reserves are found. These smaller companies have shorter time horizons than their larger counterparts, as they expect to be bought by the big players once they discover reserves. So juniors tend to devote fewer resources and effort to the development of long-term environmental and social policies or long-lasting community relations, because they do not expect to spend long periods of time in the area. Their goal is to get quick profits. The comparative advantage of juniors is their capacity to enter and leave an oil area relatively easily and their willingness to operate in high-risk areas such as the Amazon jungle, in the hope of finding large reserve pools that they can then sell to the majors at a profit. This touch-and-go operating style allows juniors to take more social and environmental risks than their larger counterparts.

The way large and small oil companies operate is not exclusive to this industry, and it is probably more frequent in other extractive industries such as mining. The world became aware of this differentiated operating style in the case of the thirty-three miners who were trapped for seventy days in a mine in Chile in 2010 as a result of safety negligence by the small-scale company operating the mine (MacNamara and Webber 2010). The different operating styles of majors and juniors becomes even more important in countries like Peru, Ecuador, and Colombia, where exploration projects are multiplying and at the beginning most new oil operators are juniors, particularly in high risk areas like the Amazon. A considerable number of conflicts originate during the initial exploration phase, and once juniors leave and larger companies come into the picture to start out the production phase, frustration among the community has likely already developed. This is a consequence of juniors largely overlooking the adoption of effective community-relations policies to minimize the negative effects of their operations. Addressing differences from early on, rather than letting them build up, would greatly reduce the potential for disputes and large-scale conflicts down the line. Luckily, as image-conscious corporations become more engaged in expanding their social and environmental practices and in cleaning up their previous record in this respect, in the past few years they have started to scrutinize more closely the behavior of juniors when assessing the long-term risk of buying oil reserves from them. As of 2012 a large number of the oil developments in the three countries were in the exploration phase, the prerogative of juniors willing to take larger risks.

Majors have become rare in the upstream of the countries being analyzed. The only large corporation operating by 2010 in the Amazon jungle was ConocoPhillips, and it was not immune to the junior company syndrome. Conoco entered the area by buying concessions in 2006—five in Peru and two in Ecuador—from a junior company, Burlington Resources, which left a controversial social and environmental record. Conoco inherited a history of conflicts, including accusations that Burlington had manipulated local Indigenous communities and violated their human rights. When Conoco came into the picture, the disputes were well advanced, particularly in Ecuador's two blocks— 23 and 24—where the new company was forced to put oil developments on hold in response to the continued opposition of local Indigenous communities. Subsequently, Conoco was accused by NGOs and shareholders of lacking a specific Indigenous policy and of failing to provide mechanisms for implementing the human rights principles it endorsed publicly (Anderson et al. 2009).

Oil reserves that are still undeveloped and high oil prices that offset the risks of exploring for them in sensitive environmental and social areas like the Amazon are an attractive combination for smaller companies. Some of them decide to stay for the long term after the exploration phase. Some juniors operating in the Amazon have shown impressive growth, although output remains low in comparative terms. Two of the most successful juniors in the region are Pacific Rubiales Energy Corporation and Petrominerales Limited, both with operations in Peru and Colombia. Between 2007 and 2009 Rubiales saw output jump from a mere 21,200 to 83,000 barrels of oil equivalent per day in just two years (Pacific Rubiales 2009); it became Colombia's second largest oil producer through its subsidiary, Meta Petroleum. Likewise, Petrominerales increased its annual oil output exponentially between 2005 and 2009 and saw its production grow from 1,031 to 22,400 barrels per day. This performance may not be notable in absolute terms, but the companies' annual steady growth is significant.

Of the four main oil-producing companies operating in Peru, judging by production and reserves, only one, Petrobras, has enough weight to compare its global production volumes with the world majors: Petrobras reported 2.6 million barrels of oil equivalent per day in 2010, compared with 2.75 million for Chevron and 4.45 million for ExxonMobil. Petrobras is slated to become one of the world majors in the medium term in light of its rapid growth, which will likely also mean acquiring the social and environmental standards characteristic of companies within that league. But for the moment, Petrobras's presence in Peru remains concealed behind much smaller contenders. The company occupies only second place after Pluspetrol in terms of output, acreage, and reserve ratios in that country. Pluspetrol may relinquish Block 1AB before the expiration of its contract in 2015. At that point, state-owned oil company Perupetro may become a partner in the development of Peru's largest oil area (*Gestion.pe* 2012).

Pluspetrol is an Argentine oil producer with global output of around 350,000 barrels of oil equivalent per day, which makes it a medium-sized company. It is roughly seven and a half times smaller than Petrobras. Privately owned Pluspetrol has more freedom to maneuver than partly state-owned Petrobras when it comes to deciding what social and environmental policies to apply and how much to invest in these, a factor that has contributed to lower costs and increased operational flexibility. In Peru, Pluspetrol has enormous weight as not only the number one oil producer but also as the upstream operator of the country's flagship natural gas project Camisea, which turned the Andean nation into Latin America's first liquefied natural gas exporter in 2010.

Perhaps an obvious example of the differences in corporate standards between oil majors and smaller, often privately owned corporations such as Pluspetrol is that in spite of its operational significance—not just in Peru but in the whole region—the Argentine company had until 2009 only one manager in the whole corporation in charge of its overall corporate social responsibility program. This remained the case even after the company had been exposed to conflict in its operations in the northern Peruvian Amazon Block 1AB/8.[15] Starting in 2009, after conflicts in Block 1AB/8 worsened and as Camisea fell under increasing international scrutiny, Pluspetrol decided to create various corporate social responsibility management units, amid resistance from older management that considered the additional investment to be of little worth to the company.[16] Camisea is perhaps the best example in the region of the importance that small- and medium-sized companies are acquiring. Most of the companies that run the huge Camisea development fit, at least in part, the junior company profile: U.S. company Hunt Oil, which leads the liquefied natural gas export segment of Camisea, is a (family-owned) private corporation, as are Pluspetrol and Tecpetrol in the upstream consortium.

The way the oil industry is structured around juniors and majors creates perverse incentives because juniors actually need the high risk of conflicts to justify their presence. For juniors, the more risk, the higher their value, since they have built a niche around their performance in high risk, difficult areas. The survival of juniors is normally linked to a particular project. Very often these companies are created to develop a specific area.[17] Sometimes, they will disappear once a major buys the oil or gas field. So it becomes essential for them that their concession be successful, and with that in mind there is always the temptation to take unacceptable shortcuts such as providing bribes, corrupting officials, or neglecting to invest in social programs—even when required by law—to ensure the highest possible rate of return on the project, so that it will become attractive to possible buyers (Bray 2003, 299).

This perverse incentive framework may change soon, as majors become more scrupulous in assessing the behavior of juniors they may be interested in acquiring. Large oil corporations typically engage in constant image checkups in relation to social, political, and environmental problems, and this practice may also extend to the juniors they acquire. For many, an example of this image cleanup is the Angola Partnership Initiative that Chevron launched in 2002 to help the African country's postconflict economic development and peacebuilding plans, after twenty-seven years of a bloody civil war that left an estimated half a million dead. Chevron is an oil pioneer in Angola, where it drilled the country's first onshore well more than fifty years ago and discovered its first offshore oil and gas field. Chevron's Angola philanthropic efforts were seen by many as an attempt to clean up its image after headaches in Ecuador, where it has been accused of polluting the Amazon during oil operations there in the 1970s.

Another example of corporate image laundering is Royal Dutch Shell, which discovered the giant Camisea natural gas reserves in Peru in the 1980s, in partnership with then Mobile Corporation. When Shell came to Peru it was an image-battered company after two catastrophes in Nigeria (*Sunday Times* 1995) and in the North Sea (Agence France Press 1991). For Shell, Camisea became its redeeming project. The company made a public commitment to adopt the highest environmental and social standards and the principle of social net benefit, by which areas affected by a project should be better off once the project is finished. Even the company's strongest critics said Shell showed an unprecedented level of social and environmental commitment (Ross 2008, 226). Shell's desire to drastically improve its image produced an exemplary social and environmental design for developing Camisea that continued to be implemented by the companies that took over the project after Shell left in 1998. However, once Shell was gone, Camisea was not devoid of conflict.

The Contract of the Century

Given the importance of Camisea for Peru and the region as a whole, the project's conflict performance deserves attention. The project was portrayed as the key to Peru's future energy and economic growth, so much so that it became known as the Contract of the Century. The year 2004 marked a turning point in Peru's energy history. In September of that year, the giant Camisea natural gas field started production for supplying the domestic market. Later, exports of liquefied natural gas by 2010 turned Peru into Latin America's first exporter of that product, switching the status of the country from a gas importer to a net exporter. The Camisea reserves are located deep in the Amazon jungle, in the Lower Urubamba region. According to some estimates, Camisea's contribution to Peru's gross domestic product exceeded US$4 billion in the period 2000–2006 and is expected to be higher than US$11 billion between 2007 and 2033 (Zavala, Guadalupe Gómez, and Carrillo Hidalgo 2007).

With Shell at its helm, the original consortium had spent some US$250 million to develop the gas field before leaving Peru in July 1998 due to disagreements with the government (*New York Times* 1998). Camisea was not developed

BOX 2   Technical facts about Camisea

Camisea gas is produced mainly from six wells: San Martin 1 and 3 and Cashiriari 1 and 3 in Block 88; and Pagoreni A and B in adjacent Block 56. Gas is piped to the Malvinas plant—producing 450 million cubic feet per day—built on the right bank of the Urubamba River. Most of Block 88 sits in the Nahua-Kugapakori Territorial Reserve, home to several indigenous populations, including the largest group, Machiguenga, as well as Nahua, Piros, and Ashaninka, among others. There are also several indigenous groups living in voluntary isolation and around fifteen thousand people in the area.

Due to high environmental and social risks, the project was designated as an "offshore inland" development (González Guardia 2009). All the equipment and personnel needed for developing the gas fields would be brought in by helicopter or boat to avoid clearing the forest and building roads that might encourage the migration of outsiders to the Indigenous territories.

In 2000 a consortium led by Argentine oil company Pluspetrol won the rights to develop the upstream component of the project for a forty-year period. The downstream segment went to another consortium, Transportadora de Gas del Peru, led by Tecgas, which received a thirty-three-year contract to transport gas and gas liquids from the Camisea reserves in the Amazon to the capital city of Lima and to the Pacific coast. Tecgas is fully owned by the Techint Group, Latin America's largest steel-making company and a world leader in the manufacture of seamless steel tubes (Zavala, Gómez, and Carrillo Hidalgo 2007). In 2002 the French-Belgian company Tractebel won the rights to distribute natural gas in the city of Lima and its environs.

In 2003 the Inter-American Development Bank approved a US$135 million loan—a $75 million fourteen-year direct credit plus a $60 million syndicated loan—for the construction of the transportation phase of the gas pipelines. On the spot, the bank embarked in unprecedented steps to adopt the highest possible level of monitoring and civil society participation in Camisea and made a public commitment to publish all documentation related to the project. It also demanded from the government and the companies involved an improvement of their policies toward the environment and Indigenous Peoples. The conditions for granting the downstream loan included an unusual and innovative requirement for the upstream consortium to be in line with the bank's social and environmental terms. If the upstream consortium failed to meet the bank's stringent demands, then the downstream operators would be in breach of the loan agreement as well.

until the beginning of the twenty-first century. Shell had sown the seeds of what could turn into a model social and environmental project not only for Peru but also for the world. The Camisea project was to be the example of solid social and environmental policies that were to be followed by future oil and gas projects in Peru's Amazon and in Latin America as a whole. At least, that is how it was presented at the time.

After Shell left, its followers had the opportunity to become known for implementing Shell's commendable model, or, on the contrary, they could stand out for not being able to follow the high standards set by the Dutch company. The private consortium that took over from Shell kept some of the company's environmental and social standards, such as burying the pipelines underground, replanting the surface with native seedlings, and treating the upstream development as "offshore" so that no access roads were built. Unfortunately, however, Camisea suffered five spills in less than a year, which tarnished the project's performance and created considerable resentment among the population (*La República* 2006). In addition to the spills, uncertain projections about the future availability of natural gas for domestic consumption led to opposition to gas exports for fear of future domestic shortages.

The Camisea project is a good example of how large corporations, such as Shell, can be effective in reducing or preventing conflict by establishing effective company policies. Camisea also shows that pressure from environmentally and socially sensitive consumers in the developed world can be key for ensuring compliance in remote areas. Fundamentally, Camisea highlights the vital role of multilateral lending institutions in ensuring that environmental and social concerns are addressed by oil investors (see box 2). These institutions have adopted increasingly stringent standards in the past fifteen years as a condition for granting loans, although many argue the standards are not high enough (Gamboa, 2008). However, in spite of the critical voices, having social and environmental demands scrutinized by outsiders is better than nothing.

A large number of the national and smaller companies entering the Latin American oil industry remain outside the international lending network. They are not subject to scrutiny by civil society organizations, so the social and environmental rules they adopt may not be the most advanced. Shareholder pressure also contributes to more stringent standards, as shareholders around the world become more conscious of the social and environmental performance of the companies they invest in, as a way of monitoring the risk of their investments. This increased interest in company performance has resulted in the development of private social and environmental rating systems such as the FTSE4 Good Socially Responsible Investment Index, which ranks companies according to environmental and social criteria. However, many of the junior or state-owned oil companies currently operating in Latin America are not publicly traded, so they are sheltered from shareholder demands for transparency.

For the junior oil companies increasingly active in Latin America, gaps in the system allow them to get away with social and environmental standards that are not high enough. Pressure from larger corporations and the international lending community are slowly starting to change this reality, but it will take some time before positive results are seen. In the meantime, conflicts keep multiplying from the initial, usually junior-managed exploration phase, and become increasingly intractable as the oil or gas development moves forward.

The final section addresses a stressor of oil conflicts unique to Colombia: four decades of armed confrontation with illegal armed groups. Colombia's armed struggle and the effect it has on hydrocarbons-related conflicts may not be extrapolated to the other two countries studied in this book. For that reason, it deserves special attention.

The Unique Stressor of Colombia's Armed Struggle

Colombia is a special case. Four decades of armed confrontation had direct effects on its oil industry, playing a major role in triggering and extending the duration of oil-related conflicts with peasant, Indigenous, and Afro-Colombian communities. Oil developments have expanded in the past decade to areas characterized by the presence of active illegal armed groups. Overall, attacks against oil infrastructure and violence in general have been reduced during that time but not totally eliminated, so they remain a source of conflict.

Oil-related conflicts in Colombia may be seen as an offshoot of the prolonged armed conflict, which goes back to the 1960s and has shown very high levels of violence. The nature of the conflict around oil in Colombia has changed with time and may be analyzed in two distinct periods. The initial phase, from the 1960s to the late 1980s, was characterized by an attempt by armed rebel groups to fill the void left within the society by an inefficient state that failed to attend to the demands of the population, especially in rural areas (Fontaine 2007c, 124–42). During this period rebels were guided by a leftist ideology, seeking power to resolve those historical grievances. The 1960s success of the Cuban Revolution was influential in expanding that ideology, and rebels found followers particularly in areas where land grabs by the well-off and their paramilitary supporters were common.

The second phase of the conflict started at the end of the Cold War, in the 1990s, when rebel groups began to see oil-producing areas with a more utilitarian objective: as a source of funds to support their war. After the Cold War most rebel movements in the region disappeared, and those that remained, particularly in Colombia, had to reinvent themselves. They no longer hoped to install a "government of the people." They now fought for their own survival, and in so doing, oil became an instrument of economic subsistence. It is not surprising, then, that following the discovery of oil in the 1980s, Colombian rebel groups strengthened and started to expand again, by using illegal practices—such as the economic extortion of foreign oil companies, and clientelistic arrangements—for capturing government oil revenues (Echandia Castilla 1998, 35–65). The practices of this second phase, guided by an economic rather than an ideological goal, support the theory of greed as a major reason for conflicts.

Both the still active Ejército de Liberación Nacional (ELN) and the largest guerrilla group, Fuerzas Armadas Revolucionarias de Colombia (FARC), have repeatedly attacked oil infrastructure and used kidnapping and extortion tactics such as the charging of "war taxes" on oil companies to finance their activities. Rebels have also been known for reaping oil royalty revenues from municipalities. In response to the guerrilla attacks, the government increased funding to military and paramilitary groups, and private security forces proliferated in the 1980s and 1990s to defend the oil infrastructure.

These parallel forces, with a mandate to protect oil infrastructure, have been known to commit illegal actions similar to the rebels'. The paramilitary has long been accused of being at the forefront of Colombia's illegal commercialization of gasoline, which they allegedly use as a source of financing (Semana.com 2002). In the northern gas-producing province of Guajira, on the border with Venezuela, paramilitary forces are said to be in control. They have been accused of illegally managing imports of gasoline from Venezuela, through brutal extortions and killings at the expense of the local population, which is dominated by the Wayuu, Colombia's largest native tribe (Kraul, 2008). Paramilitary groups often try to push guerrillas away from lucrative oil-producing areas, seeking to prevent them from extracting an oil tax from companies, which they and the military allegedly charge instead (Wirpsa and Dunning 2004). This dynamic has led to increasing violence and often abuses against the local population, as paramilitary groups in particular have been accused of committing atrocious human rights abuses against irregular armed forces, in the name of military protection. In the words of Scott Pearce (2002, 9), the paramilitary "were effectively mercenaries used to silence political opponents and preserve the economic position of their patrons." Paramilitary groups are believed to be unscrupulous in their actions. In some oil-producing areas, such as the province of Arauca, the army and paramilitary groups even joined forces with the ELN in opposition to their common enemy, the FARC (Semana.com 2009).

Violent attacks on oil infrastructure have social and environmental consequences that contribute to an extremely high toll on the population living in the oil-producing provinces. Not surprisingly, violence indicators are higher than the national average in oil-producing regions, because wherever there are oil reserves there are armed groups fighting for control, and the local civilian population is caught in between (Pearce 2002, 17). Violence has led to the massive expulsion of peasant communities from oil-producing areas, adding to the country's overall enormous numbers of displaced populations from the armed conflict. Official figures set the number of displaced persons throughout the country at a little more than three million in 2009, while civil society estimated them to be closer to four million. Back then, Colombia had the world's second-largest displaced person crisis, after Sudan (McDougall 2010, 6).

Sometimes, civilians are co-opted or forced to contribute to the cause of one group or the other. Given the daily dangers they confront, populations living in oil-producing areas often harbor deep hatred toward oil activities, which they blame for bringing violence to their lands. It is common for local populations to believe that the government and oil companies are allied in trying to take their oil-rich lands away from them and develop the resources to their advantage. In addition, rebel groups are thought to have lost much of their initial appeal among local populations that have been directly affected by their violent actions.

La Flauta

The Caño Limón oil pipeline stretches for 477 miles across eight departments, from Colombia's Caño Limón field in the northeastern department of Arauca to the Caribbean port of Coveñas. The 900,000-barrel-per-day capacity conduit is the factual emblem of Colombia's oil potential. In 1986 Colombia started exporting oil through the Caño Limón pipeline, and it was that year that the South American country entered the map of world oil-exporting nations.

Not only is Caño Limón an oil icon in Colombia, it also bears unfortunate political weight in the country's forty-year armed conflict. The pipeline became a strategic target for guerrilla groups since it first started operating almost three decades ago. In fact, Colombians call it *la flauta* (the flute) for the number of holes it withstood during various attacks throughout the years. Other pipelines have also been attacked, though less frequently (MiPutumayo.com 2011). The Colombian ombudsman reported a total of 4,101 attacks to the country's main oil transport lines between 1986 and 2001. During the same period Caño Limón was attacked 714 times, which resulted in a loss of 2.116 million barrels of oil and cost roughly US$130 million to repair (Office of the Ombudsman 2008a, 5–7). Attacks on oil infrastructure, particularly the Caño Limón, have become so frequent that state-owned oil company Ecopetrol devotes a special section of its yearly reports to information about them.

Attacks on oil infrastructure were not uncommon during the early stages of the guerrilla movement when Colombia was not yet an important producer. At the start of the guerrilla movement, in the 1960s and 1970s, the state structure was very weak and government actions were to a large extent monopolized by the two major political parties—Conservative and Liberal—that shared the power. The guerrilla movements of the time tried to capitalize on the lower echelons of the society that fell between the cracks of this unspoken power-sharing agreement among the elites. Many scholars attribute the spread of Colombia's guerrilla movement to the power dynamic between the ruling elite and the majority of poor or low middle-class origin who were excluded (Leal Buitrago 1991).

Later, in the 1980s, the rebels changed strategies and abandoned their initial goal of achieving territorial control. Instead, the insurgent groups aimed now for the control of strategic areas to ensure their economic survival (Echandia Castilla and Bechara Gómez 2006). The new discoveries of very promising oil reservoirs toward the end of the 1980s and beginning of the 1990s, and the infrastructure built around them, provided a new potential for income. As a consequence, guerrilla groups in the 1990s increased their presence in departments of strategic oil value, and violent actions started to multiply around oil installations. The ELN was especially active in the Arauca department, home to the Caño Limón field, until the end of the 1990s, when the FARC took a more active role (Vicepresidencia 2002). Tactics employed for accessing revenues included kidnappings, intimidation, attacks on infrastructure, and oil theft.

The departments of Casanare, Arauca, and Meta were the three main oil-producing areas in the country between 2007 and 2009. During those years the last two departments were centers of major armed confrontation. Even in 2009, when the armed conflict in Colombia in general showed signs of winding down, Arauca and Meta still experienced intense fighting. The Cusiana-Cupiagua fields, one of the largest oil- and gas-producing areas in Colombia, are located in the department of Casanare, where armed confrontations have been less intense than in the other two departments.

The U.S. government devoted US$99 million to fund equipment and provide training to Colombian military personnel as part of an infrastructure security strategy in the department of Arauca (U.S. Government 2005). Ecopetrol and U.S. oil company Occidental Petroleum contributed another US$8.65 million and participated in the design of community-development programs in that department. Occidental is the operator of the Caño Limón field and one of the partners in the pipeline—together with Ecopetrol and Repsol.

To protect Caño Limón from attacks, Occidental engaged the protection of the Colombian Army through the U.S.-funded program to enhance infrastructure security (U.S. Government 2005). Special army units were created and funded solely to protect oil infrastructure. The Eighteenth Army Brigade, whose coat of arms includes an armed military man and an oil well, was charged with looking after Caño Limón. While the security plan helped to reduce attacks on the Caño Limón pipeline, it also derailed when the brigade was linked to abuses in cooperation with paramilitary groups, including kidnapping and killing suspected guerrilla followers. Occidental became particularly vulnerable after news

Eighteenth Army Brigade coat of arms. Courtesy of Wikimedia Commons (2013), Creative Commons License 3.0.

reports linked the company with a violent attack on a village close to its operations in Caño Limón, where eleven adults and seven children were reported dead (Miller 2002).

The provision of oil infrastructure security has by some accounts contributed to reducing the number of guerrilla attacks on oil pipelines in general, and particularly on Caño Limón, which experienced 13 incidents in 2010, down from 170 in 2001 (Kraul 2011). On the other hand, the new infrastructure security scheme caused a shift in the type and geography of the attacks, and, most important, it opened up a whole new range of conflicts that added to Colombia's already complex armed confrontation. Increased security in the Arauca portion of the Caño Limón pipeline caused attacks to shift to the section of the line that crosses the department of Norte de Santander. In addition, there has been a change in the modality of the attacks, with more strikes on the electrical grid that feeds the pipeline, as opposed to the pipe itself (U.S. Government 2005).

One of the mechanisms for improving the security of oil infrastructure is the payment of what is known as a "war tax" or "security quotas" by companies to illegal groups to avoid attacks. This practice started a sort of witch hunt among the population in search of those linked to the groups, which soon resulted in a considerable increase of homicides, massacres, death threats, and other violent activities (United Nations General Assembly 2008). Other security mechanisms were organized around private security groups that in Colombia may include right-wing paramilitary organizations, which have historically described themselves as opposing the country's leftist guerrilla movements. At the local level hydrocarbons conflicts in Colombia show similar triggering elements as in Peru and Ecuador, such as weak consultation processes, governance inefficiencies, and legal limitations. But in practice, the armed confrontation is the main stressor of oil conflicts.

SUMMARY

The existence of stress elements mainly related to the behavior of the stakeholders involved in hydrocarbons projects may contribute to fomenting conflict. Sometimes, when these stressors are not resolved in a timely manner, the disputes tend to become violent or to drag out over time. All actors involved in oil and gas conflicts have a responsibility to try to solve disputes, because each one usually contributes, directly or indirectly, to the buildup of the circumstances that lead to the conflict.

Sometimes, divisions within Indigenous communities, or between communities and their umbrella organization, prevent the development of a united front with respect to an oil project, resulting in conflictive relations. Similarly, differences among members of the civil society active in a specific oil-producing area or agendas of NGOs that do not quite reflect local needs may end up exacerbating the conflict. Likewise, when oil companies fail to adopt sound social and environmental safeguards, local communities react and their frustrations may lead to conflict. In the same vein, in the absence of development projects designed in a participatory way for the benefit of the communities affected by the oil project, oil or gas revenues may be misspent, which in turn may lead to conflict.

What differentiates the conflict stressors described in this chapter from the structural flaws analyzed in chapter 3 is that in the case of the former solutions can be more readily available and easier to apply if the parties involved in the conflict are willing to do so. Conflict mitigation may be achieved more rapidly than in the presence of structural flaws, which call for more complex and deeper institutional changes. The presence of credible institutional mediation goes a long way in mitigating the conflict stressors described in this chapter in a relatively short period. Assertive government involvement in every stage of the oil project from the beginning can contribute to conflict prevention by granting a sense of legitimacy to the project while reducing the feeling of isolation among the community. Having an in-depth knowledge of the context in which the conflict developed is a must for trying to solve or prevent disputes. But in the end, finding a permanent solution to a dispute typically depends on the readiness of the stakeholders involved to take the necessary steps in that direction.

CONCLUSION

FROM 2000 TO 2010 Latin America experienced an unprecedented increase in the number of conflicts related to natural resources in general and oil and gas in particular. This tendency has been especially pronounced in Peru, and to a lesser extent in Ecuador and Colombia. Many of the disputes were related to oil and natural gas reserves located in the Amazon basin and its surrounding areas, home to large numbers of Indigenous Peoples. These historically marginalized groups have for years maintained numerous grievances that have largely gone unnoticed by the rest of the population. A rapidly developing and increasingly assertive movement of Indigenous Peoples across Latin America is demanding improved living conditions, more political representation, and recognition of their specific cultural identity. They are questioning the benefits of the proliferation of oil and gas developments in the areas they inhabit and are increasingly demanding a fair share of the profits. Their struggle for acceptance has been further legitimized by growing international appreciation of their cultural uniqueness and recognition of their rights.

In this context, local conflicts around extractive industries in the Amazon carry a political significance that goes far beyond ensuring an equitable distribution of economic benefits. The growing number of local conflicts related to oil and gas development opens up a broad range of unresolved questions that have cultural, political, and economic dimensions: How will Indigenous populations be integrated in Latin American societies in the future? What will be the terms of the social contract currently being reshaped between Indigenous communities and the rest of society? Are governments and Latin American societies ready to recognize the cultural and economic distinctiveness of the various Indigenous communities living in large extensions of their territory, even if this recognition might mean a redefinition or change of approach to natural resource development?

Our study recognizes that the volatile political dimension of oil-related conflicts makes it difficult to find definitive answers to questions and to solve disputes. However, our research identified several areas for improving the performance of state institutions and for adopting more efficient management practices in the oil and gas industries that could go a long way in mitigating conflicts in a relatively short time frame, including the participation of a well-respected entity to facilitate dialogue; the implementation of participatory mechanisms for designing local development projects; the optimization of the process of oil revenue distribution; and the completion of social and environmental mappings of the areas to be developed prior to the granting of licenses. These steps could occur while long-term political decisions related to the inclusion of Indigenous communities are being considered and discussed.

Our research identifies various causes of oil- and gas-related conflicts, which we have divided in two groups. The first group consists of structural flaws embedded in the institutional and legal framework of the three countries under review. The second group includes stressors from the group dynamics of the stakeholders involved that contribute to escalating the conflicts. This second group of conflict stressors is easier to address, as long as the stakeholders involved are ready to agree on modifying certain patterns of behavior and actions that exacerbate the disputes.

By contrast, resolving the structural flaws that contribute to conflicts is complex and time consuming. It would entail the reform of institutional and legal systems that have been accepted and applied, even if ineffectively, by a wide variety of stakeholders for decades. Furthermore, modifying these structural flaws would in some cases call for a political commitment to reform that societies may not be ready to make. Among these stubborn institutional flaws, the decentralization process adopted by the three countries studied in this research incorporates some of the most pressing governance failures that need to be addressed, in particular poor local management of new oil revenues, corruption and clientelistic behavior within local governments, the weak presence of the central government in oil and gas development areas, and miscommunication or poor coordination between different government agencies in charge of local social and economic development processes. Fiscal decentralization has often transferred the governance flaws of the central administration to the regional or local areas where the oil or gas projects are being developed. These effects of the decentralization process need to be rapidly addressed to prevent them from spreading further through the different subnational government levels.

The legal framework that governs the oil and gas industries is also highly problematic. Often poorly implemented, laws can overlap or become overabundant. They are also frequently modified to accommodate short-term needs.

Legal mechanisms for solving hydrocarbons disputes can be convoluted and slow, and not always effective. Most important, the countries studied for this research lack effective local and territorial planning for defining areas that may be apt for oil or gas development and those that should be protected due to their social or environmental characteristics. All of this contributes to the intensification of local conflicts and to a generalized tendency to bring disputes to international courts rather than domestic tribunals, with the hope of achieving faster resolution abroad.

There is still an opportunity for obtaining a relatively rapid beneficial impact by addressing the more transient, second group of conflict stressors. Our research found examples of changes in attitudes, or in the modus operandi of stakeholders, that contributed to mitigating the intensity of oil conflicts. In Ecuador, for example, the adoption of a unified front by the Indigenous movement resulted in a positive resolution of conflictive situations with regard to oil developments. Likewise, sound corporate practices and sustained supervision by multilateral institutions of Peru's Camisea natural gas project ensured relatively high social and environmental safeguards from the start and resulted in the long-term establishment of effective conflict management practices. Another relatively straightforward step that could contribute to reducing or containing the number of conflicts in the short term is the involvement of recognized institutions, or even personalities, that enjoy a solid popular backing to act as mediators. The best example of a positive institutional intervention in the region is that of Peru's Office of the Ombudsman, whose actions have been praised for success in resolving disputes and in some cases averting conflicts altogether by creating a space for dialogue. In the same vein, various rulings by Colombia's Constitutional Court that ensured adequate attention to the claims of Indigenous communities had important beneficial impacts in settling or even preventing oil conflicts.

This is not to say that addressing the second group of conflict stressors is a simple process, devoid of difficulties. But it is a good first step that could have tangible results in a relatively short period, particularly if instituted as a preventive measure prior to a conflict. Early action could help to challenge the perception of abandonment among the affected population, while contributing alternative solutions to differences of opinion. Once a conflict has developed, it is difficult to defuse. Instead, with the adoption of early conflict alert signals, disputes might be avoided or mitigated through the mechanisms set in motion prior to the conflict. Overall, however, we found that there is still a lack of a general commitment to devote enough effort, financial resources, and political will to address this second group of conflict triggers in a way that could have rapid, short-term results. This reluctance is even greater with regard to adopting a conflict-prevention agenda prior to an actual dispute.

Conflict-prevention policies adopted when the oil or gas projects are being designed are key for avoiding large-scale disputes during the exploration or production phases of the project. A solid conflict-prevention policy should build on a detailed understanding of the social and cultural framework that characterizes the project's area of influence. Conflicts related to oil and gas are usually influenced by the historical, social, and cultural context of the population most affected by the project. Memories of past contamination or noncompliance by previous stakeholders, a history of local opposition to oil projects, or the knowledge of past grievances expressed by a nearby community may foreshadow strong opposition to oil or gas activities in a specific territory. Natural resource conflicts are largely influenced by perceptions, which are to a large extent defined through the lens of these factors. Often, conflicts break out when a community perceives future risks in being exposed to an oil or gas project, long before an actual threat from the project materializes. A thorough understanding early on of the sociocultural and historical framework that surrounds an oil or gas project is essential to build early dispute-prevention mechanisms.

Not all stakeholders carry the same weight when it comes to influencing the development of oil or gas conflicts. The role of the central government is unique and can serve to mitigate conflicts, but it can also have the insidious effect of triggering more disputes if the issues that started the differences are not properly and promptly addressed. Oil-related conflicts may be exacerbated by action or inaction on the part of the central government. Conflicts may come as a consequence of decisions on the part of the authorities contrary to the wishes of the communities. But it is very common for disputes to escalate when there is not enough central government involvement, precisely due to frustration among the affected population, which feels abandoned by the state. Conflict-prevention mechanisms in place before the start-up of oil or gas activities in a particular area can help to address this feeling of neglect.

The involvement of central government authorities during negotiations between local communities and oil companies is essential for various reasons, among them to ensure that rules and regulations are respected, to grant legitimacy to the process, to act as arbiters when differences arise, or simply to send a message of recognition to largely forgotten communities. Our review of cases shows that the absence of the central authorities in these situations is often an important contributor to conflicts.

The behavior of the other stakeholders can also act as a conflict stressor within the second group of oil-related triggers. The type of companies involved and the social responsibility policies they adopt may tilt the balance toward the resolution or the aggravation of differences. The Western majors that were historically the main players in the oil and gas industries worldwide have been gradually giving way to state-owned counterparts or to smaller players that sometimes have questionable environmental and social practices. This research has plenty of examples of the effect on the development of oil conflicts from diverse social and environmental corporate attitudes. Likewise, the degree of activism of communities affected by hydrocarbons projects and the style of action adopted by the civil society involved in the area both play a fundamental role in the development of oil conflicts.

Our study has identified a number of reforms and actions that we believe could address the second group of more transient conflict triggers and could contribute to solutions for oil- and gas-related conflicts in these countries in a relatively short period. Among these is the adoption of well-designed territorial planning to identify areas that may be open to extractive activities and regions that should remain shielded from such activity. This mapping of extractive areas within the borders of a particular country could be used as the basis for long-term decisions by all the stakeholders, particularly with regard to the granting of oil or gas concessions.

Another important action for mitigating oil conflicts would be to ensure the improvement of existing revenue distribution mechanisms so that oil profits make their way back to the producing regions. Parallel to that, local development projects to be funded with the new oil income should be designed early on in a transparent way, with the participation of local communities. This action would strengthen the local government's accountability in the design and implementation of local development policies. In this context, the authorities should also monitor that social actions taken by companies remain within the framework of the development plans previously designed locally with the participation of the affected communities. This would guarantee that responsibility for the plans and for monitoring their implementation are evenly shared among the different actors.

An analysis of available institutional mediation in the three countries researched for this book show that Peru and Colombia have relatively effective mechanisms for addressing oil- and gas-related conflicts. The Peruvian Office of the Ombudsman and the Constitutional Court of Colombia can both serve as inspiration for the incorporation of agile and effective elements to institutional mediation mechanisms, which could in turn help to reduce the number and intensity of oil-related conflicts. Both institutions are generally well regarded by local communities affected by oil projects, and this is an essential condition for their successful intervention. Ensuring the existence of clear consultation policies and well-designed laws and regulations, and their proper implementation by all stakeholders, would greatly contribute to mitigating oil-related conflicts. Our analysis shows that existing consultation mechanisms are not as effective as they should be in the countries we studied, and that is a constant source of conflict. Perhaps the foundations of the consultation process as stated by the ILO Convention 169 should be revisited to make the process more effective.

Our research also shows that smaller junior oil companies do not always adequately apply appropriate social and environmental safeguards when operating in the three countries under review. Monitoring of their operations should be reinforced, perhaps through the development of a peer review mechanism among companies, that could serve to detect flaws in the system of safeguards. Finally, coordinated efforts should be geared toward strengthening the capacity of the Indigenous Peoples movement so that they may effectively contribute to company monitoring and improve their proficiency during complex negotiations and legal proceedings with companies.

These recommendations are obviously not easy to implement. Our case studies show that they must be adapted to each specific country and local context for them to be successful in the long term. Most important, a comprehensive commitment to these recommendations from the various actors involved would be necessary to guarantee their success. The violence shown during some recent conflicts, particularly the Bagua events in Peru in 2009, evidences the potential destabilizing force of these disputes unless they are properly and swiftly addressed. This is particularly true given Latin American countries' imperfect and still relatively fragile institutions and their recent history of bloody rebel movements.

NOTES

Introduction

1. There is no universal definition of "Indigenous Peoples." This book adopts the most commonly cited definition by José R. Martinez Cobo, the special rapporteur of the Sub-Commission on Prevention of Discrimination and Protection of Minorities. Cobo defines Indigenous communities, peoples, and nations as "those which, having a historical continuity with pre-invasion and pre-colonial societies that developed on their territories, consider themselves distinct from other sectors of the societies now prevailing in those territories, or parts of them. They form at present nondominant sectors of society and are determined to preserve, develop and transmit to future generations their ancestral territories, and their ethnic identity, as the basis of their continued existence as peoples, in accordance with their own cultural patterns, social institutions and legal systems" (1987, 7 adds. 1–4).

2. The term *hydrocarbons* refers to both oil and gas.

3. Among some of the classic works that make a connection between civil war and natural resources are Bannon and Collier (2003) and Ballentine and Nitzschke (2005).

4. The Bolivarian Alliance for the Americas was created by Chávez in 2004 as an alternative to U.S.-sponsored trade relations in the hemisphere. Member countries include Cuba, Bolivia, and Ecuador.

5. Departments in Latin America are equivalent to states in the United States.

Chapter 1. Tracing Oil- and Gas-Related Conflicts

1. OPEC is an intergovernmental organization formed by the world's largest oil-producing countries responsible for some 40 percent of world oil production. Of its twelve member countries, half are from the Middle East: Iran, Iraq, Kuwait, Qatar, Saudi Arabia, and United Arab Emirates. Among the rest there are four from Africa: Algeria, Angola, Nigeria, and Libya; and two from South America: Venezuela and Ecuador.

2. The definition of nonconventional oil in this book refers to crude that is not easily found and that usually requires more costly techniques than conventional oil to be extracted.

3. Peru's national census does not identify or quantify its population according to ethnic or Indigenous origins, but only with regard to its native language. Indigenous

Peoples are not recognized as such by Peruvian law, as they were merged into farming communities in the Andes and the coast and native communities in the Amazon. This creates a vacuum of information that probably explains the large disparities of the percentages of the population considered Indigenous: 13 percent versus 30 percent according to official and nonofficial figures, respectively (UNICEF-FUNPROEIB Andes 2009).

4. The name in Spanish of the first oil worker's union was Sociedad Union Obrera, which later became Union Sindical Obrera.

5. Initially, the Negritos and Lobitos fields were owned by two UK companies: London and Pacific Petroleum, and Lobitos Oilfields, respectively. They were later bought by Standard Oil in 1913. Zorritos was operated by a company called Piaggio, which had been created by an immigrant merchant who settled in Callao on the Pacific coast.

6. Ecuador left OPEC in 1992 and returned in 2007.

7. In 1974 and 1975 decrees 2310 and 743 excluded private investments in the oil industry. The decrees established that only Ecopetrol would be allowed to explore and develop oil in the future, either on its own or in association with other companies.

8. Decree 1760 passed in 2003 created the Agencia Nacional de Hidrocarburos, and Law 1118 passed in 2006 authorized the partial privatization of Ecopetrol. The company sold 10 percent of its shares in an initial public offering in 2007.

9. These laws include the Law of Foreign Investment (Ley de la Inversión Extranjera), Legislative Decree 662; the Framework Law for the Increase of Private Investment (Ley Marco para el Crecimiento de la Inversión Privada), Legislative Decree 757; and the Law for the Promotion of Private Investment in Public Service Infrastructure Work (Ley de Promoción a la Inversión Privada en Obras Públicas de Infraestructura de Servicios Públicos, TUO approved by Supreme Decree 059-96-PCM (Proinversión 2011).

Chapter 2. Indigenous Peoples and Natural Resource Development

1. Particularly innovative were three Constitutional Court rulings concerning customary law in relation to Indigenous groups, pursuant to Article 246 of the 1991 Constitution. This article delegates the exercise of judicial functions to authorities within native territorial areas, in accordance to their own rules and procedures, as long as these are not contrary to the constitution and laws of the republic. According to the constitution, the law has to establish the forms of coordination of this special Indigenous jurisdiction with the national judicial system.

2. The UN Declaration on the Rights of Indigenous Peoples was adopted by General Assembly Resolution 61/295 on September 13, 2007. Initially, a total of 143 countries voted in favor, 4 against, and 11 abstained. The 4 states that opposed it were Australia, Canada, New Zealand, and the United States. Australia finally endorsed the declaration in 2009; and New Zealand, the United States, and Canada did so in 2010.

3. The Gini coefficient is a number between zero and one that measures the degree of income inequality in a given society. A zero coefficient reflects a society where everyone receives exactly the same share, and a level one coefficient is when one member would get all the income and the rest none.

Chapter 3. Structural Causes of Local Conflicts

1. Law 27506 of 2001, known as "Canon Law," established the distribution of natural resource revenues among regional and local governments. Supreme Decree 005-2002-EF, passed in 2002, developed six different types of Canon to be charged according to the various natural resource-based economic activities: mining, gas, oil, hydroelectric power, forestry and fishing.

2. The three departments receive 45 percent of all royalty revenues in the following proportion: Casanare (70 percent), Arauca (60 percent), and Meta (20 percent). Decree 1747 of 1995 established the following minimum goals: 1 percent infant mortality; 100 percent basic health coverage; 90 percent access to education; and 70 percent supply of drinking water.

3. Two of the main laws governing national parks extensively address the issue of Indigenous protected areas—the Law 2 of 1959: Which Dictates Norms for the Nation's Forestry Economics and Renewable Natural Resource Conservation (Por el Cual se Dictan Normas sobre Economía Forestal de la Nación y Conservación de Recursos Naturales Renovables); and Decree 2811 of 1974: Which Dictates the National Code of Renewable Natural Resources and Environmental Protection (Por el Cual se Dicta el Código Nacional de Recursos Naturales Renovables y de Protección al Medio Ambiente), from Colombia's 1991 Constitution and its 2005 amendments, arts. 63, 286, 287, 329, 330.

4. Interview with Indigenous leader in Iquitos, Peru, March 2010.

5. Supreme Decree 017-96-AG, published on October 19, 1996, implements article 7 of Law 26505. The decree was modified by Supreme Decree 015-2003-AG, published on May 7, 2003.

6. Interview with Oleoducto de Crudos Pesados (OCP) official, April 2010.

7. Inter-American Convention on Human Rights, Pact of San José, Costa Rica, B-32, art. 21; IACHR 2012, arts. 341.2, 341.3, 341.4 (translation by author).

8. IACHR 2012, art. 220 (translation by author).

Chapter 4. Transient Triggers of Local Conflicts

1. In 1991 Judith Kimberling wrote *Amazon Crude*, a book that became the first written chronicle about the environmental and social effects of the Texaco oil development

in Ecuador. Around that time, the campaign Amazonía por la Vida was organized by various national and international environmental organizations to protect the Amazon forest.

2. Interview with Talisman representatives, Peru, February 2010.

3. Interview with Pitiur Unti Saant, leader from the Achuar community and elder from Unkum, a community that lives in the area of Block 64, close to the Ecuadorean border, where Talisman was exploring for oil, March 2010.

4. The International Labor Organization Indigenous and Tribal Peoples in Independent Countries Convention 169 came into force in 1991. Peru's 1993 ratification is Legislative Resolution No. 26253; Colombia's 1991 ratification is Law 21; and Ecuador's 1998 ratification was Executive Decree 1387. The UN declaration came into force in 2007.

5. For Ecuador, see the National Constitution (2008), arts. 57, 398, 407; Executive Decree 1040 (2008); Environmental Law 37 (1999), art. 28. For Colombia, see Law 21 (1991); Law 99 (1993); Decree 1320 (1998); Decree 200 (2003); Decree 1220 (2005). For Peru, see Law 26300 (modified by Supreme Decrees 002-2009, 012-2008-EM, and 015-2006, and Ministerial Resolution 571-2008); Supreme Decree 012-2008 EM (2008); Consultation Law (2010); Law 28611 (2005).

6. See United Nations (2007), arts. 10, 11(2), 19, 28(1), 29(2), and 32(2).

7. For Peru, see Supreme Decree 046-93-EM, passed in 1993. For Colombia, see Law 99, passed in 1993, and Decree 1220, passed in 2005. For Ecuador, see Executive Decree 1215, passed in 2001.

8. Citizen participation in hydrocarbons activities in Peru is defined by several laws and regulations: Lineamientos para la Participación Ciudadana en las Actividades de Hidrocarburos, Ministerial Resolution 571-2008-MEM-DM; Reglamento de Protección Ambiental en las Actividades de Hidrocarburos, Supreme Decree 015-2006-EM; Reglamento de Participación Ciudadana para la Realización de Actividades de Hidrocarburos, Supreme Decree 012-2008-EM: and ILO Convention 169.

9. Interviews with various government officials, Lima, Iquitos, Madre de Dios, 2007–11.

10. Interview with Beatriz Merino, ombudsman, New York, April 2009.

11. Indigenous federations located on the border with Ecuador and Colombia opposed the arrival of Brazilian oil company Petrobras to develop Block 117, located in their territory (Office of the Ombudsman 2009a, 253).

12. The gas plant belongs to the Consorcio Terminales GMT-Terminal Ilo. The contamination fears were related to Block 155, located in the province of Moho, where Argentine oil company Pluspetrol has an oil development license (Office of the Ombudsman 2009a, 259).

13. Usually the term "major" refers to the largest privately owned oil companies in terms of production and reserves, revenues, market capitalization, and cash flow. Today, those companies include Chevron (United States), BP (United Kingdom), ExxonMobil

(United Kingdom), Total (French), Royal Dutch Shell (United Kingdom and Holland), and Conoco (United States).

14. Interview with company officials, Ecuador, March, 2010.

15. Blocks 8/8x and 1AB were transferred from Occidental Petroleum to Pluspetrol in 1996 and 2001, respectively.

16. Interviews with company officials, Buenos Aires, 2009–10.

17. Colombia's second largest producing company, Meta Petroleum Limited, was created to develop oil specifically from the Rubiales and the Piriri oil fields in Colombia's Llanos basin.

BIBLIOGRAPHY

Agence France Press. 1991. "Shell Oil Suffering Serious Image Problems: British Official." June 11.

Alvarado, Genaro. 2009. "Nativos toman lotes petroleros y un aeropuerto de Pluspetrol." *La Republica*, June 8. http://www.larepublica.pe/bagua-masacre/08/06/2009 /nativos-toman-Blocks-petroleros-y-un-aeropuerto-de-pluspetrol.

Alvaro, Mercédes. 2009. "Ecuador: Talks with China on $1 Billion Loan Suspended." *Dow Jones Newswire*. Quito, November 12.

Anaya, James. 2009. "International Human Rights and Indigenous Peoples: The Move toward the Multicultural State." Discussion Paper 09-34, Arizona Legal Studies. Tucson: University of Arizona, James E. Rogers College of Law.

———. 2005. "Avances en la era contemporánea de los derechos humanos." In *Los pueblos indígenas en el derecho internacional*, 99. Madrid: Trotta / Universidad Internacional de Andalucia.

Anderson, Mitch, Mat Finer, Daniel Herriges, Andrew Miller, and Atossa Soltani. 2009. *Conoco Phillips in the Peruvian Amazon: A Report by Amazon Watch and Save America's Forests*. Washington, D.C.: Amazon Watch and Save America's Forests.

Andrade Echeverría, Marco. 2010. *De la serpiente tecnológica a la mariposa de las secuoyas: El proyecto OCP y la ecología política del conflicto*. Quito: FLACSO Sede Ecuador; Abya Yala.

Arellano-Yanguas, Javier. 2008. "A Thoroughly Modern Resource Curse? The New Natural Resource Policy Agenda and the Mining Revival in Peru." Working Paper 300. Brighton, U.K.: Center for the Future State, Institute of Development Studies, University of Sussex.

Asociación Colombiana de Petróleo. 2013. "Informe Estadístico Petrolero." Bogotá: Asociación Colombiana de Petróleo, May 22.

Atal, Juan Pablo, Hugo Nopo, and Natalia Winder. 2009. *New Century, Old Disparities: Gender and Ethnic Wage Gaps in Latin America*. Washington, D.C.: Inter-American Development Bank.

Avellaneda Cusaria, José Alfonso. 2004. "Petróleo, ambiente y conflicto en Colombia." In *Guerra, sociedad y medio ambiente*, edited by Mauricio Cardenas, 464–501. Bogotá: Foro Nacional Ambiental.

Ballentine, Karen, and Heiko Nitzschke, eds. 2005. *Profiting from Peace: Managing the Resource Dimension of Civil War*. Boulder: Lynne Rienner.

Banco Central del Ecuador. *Estadísticas Macroeconómicas*. 2011. http://www.bce.fin.ec /frame.php?CNT=ARB0000019.

——. 2006. *Dirección general de estudios*. Vol. 2 of *Análisis de sector petrolero: IV trimestre 2006*. Quito: Banco Central del Ecuador.

——. 2005. *Memoria Annual 2005*. Quito: Banco Central del Ecuador.

Bannon, Ian, and Paul Collier, eds. 2003. *Natural Resources and Violent Conflict: Options and Actions*. Washington, D.C.: World Bank.

Barthelemy, Francoise. 2003. "Las transnacionales del petróleo al asalto." *Le Monde Diplomatique*, Cono Sur ed., January: 8–9.

BBC News. 2011. "Chevron Fined for Amazon Pollution by Ecuador Court." *Latin America and Caribbean News*. February 15. http://www.bbc.co.uk/news/world-latin -america-12460333. Accessed February 15, 2011.

——. 2009. "'Many Missing' after Peru Riots." June 8. http://news.bbc.co.uk/2/hi /americas/8088350.stm. Accessed November 14, 2011.

Bello, Alvaro. 2008. "Los pueblos indígenas y las contradicciones de la globalización." In *Globalización, derechos humanos y pueblos indígenas*, edited by Alvaro Bello and José Aylwin Oyarzun, 48–65. Temuco: Biblioteca del Congreso Nacional de Chile.

Bernal, Raquel, and Mauricio Cardenas. 2005. "Race and Ethnic Inequality in Health and Health Care in Colombia." Working Paper Series. Bogotá: Fedesarrollo.

BP. 2011. *Statistical Review of World Energy, June 2011*. London: BP.

——. 2010. *Statistical Review of World Energy, 2010*. London: BP.

——. 2009. *Statistical Review of World Energy, 2009*. London: BP.

——. 2003–11. *Sustainability Review*. London: BP.

Bray, John. 2003. "Attracting Reputable Companies to Risky Environments: Petroleum and Mining Companies." In *Natural Resources and Violent Conflict: Options and Actions*, edited by Ian Bannon and Paul Collier, 287–352. Washington, D.C.: World Bank.

Business Monitor International. 2010. "Quito Looks to China for US$1 Billion Loan for Oil Swap." *America's Oil and Gas Insights*, August 1.

Calle Valladares, Isabel, and Iván Brehaut. 2007. *Manual educativo: El ABC de las áreas naturales protegidas y la superposición de lotes de hidrocarburos*. Lima: Sociedad Peruana de Derecho Ambiental.

Carbonnier, Gilles, Fritz Brugger, and Jana Krause. 2011. "Global and Local Policy Responses to the Resource Trap." *Global Governance: A Review of Multilateralism and International Organizations*, April–June: 247–64.

CEACR (Committee of Experts on the Application of Conventions and Recommendations). 2010. "Individual Observation concerning Indigenous and Tribal Peoples

Convention, 1989 (No. 169) Peru (Ratification: 1994)." In *Monitoring Indigenous and Tribal Peoples' Rights through Conventions. A Compilation of ILO Supervisory Bodies' Comments, 2009–2010*, 106–17. Program to Promote ILO Convention 169 (PROL) 169. Geneva: International Labor Standards Department, International Labor Organization.

CEPAL (Comisión Económica para América Latina). 2010. *La inversión extranjera directa en América Latina y el Caribe, 2010*. Santiago: Naciones Unidas.

———. 2009. "Panorama regional de la inversión extranjera directa en América Latina y el Caribe." In *La inversión extranjera directa en América Latina y el Caribe, 2009*, 27–85. Santiago: Naciones UnidasCEPAL.

Cepeda Espinosa, Manuel José. 2006. "How Far May Colombia's Constitutional Court Go to Protect IDP Rights?" *Forced Migration Review*, December.

Chapin, Mac. 2004. "A Challenge to Conservationists." World Watch Institute 17, no. 6 (November–December): 17–31.

Chevron. 2003–11. *Corporate Responsibility Reports*. San Ramon, Calif.: Chevron Corporation. http://www.chevron.com/news/publications/#b3. Accessed March 7, 2013.

Chiriff, Alberto. 2010. "Los achuares del Corrientes: El estado ante su propio paradigma." *Anthropologica* 28: 289–309.

Collier, Paul. 2007. *The Bottom Billion: Why the Poorest Countries Are Failing and What Can Be Done about It*. Oxford: Oxford University Press.

El Comercio.com. 2010. "Cuatro petroleras empreden la retirada." November 26. http://www.elcomercio.com/negocios/petroleras-emprended-retirada_0_379162090.html.

———. 2008. "Agip reanuda bombeo de crudo, pero la recuperación será lenta." April 1. http://www.elcomercio.com/solo_texto_search.asp?id_noticia=117607&anio=2008&mes=4&dia=1.

———. 2007a. "Agip y amazónicos, no firman un convenio." February 13. http://www.elcomercio.com/solo_texto_search.asp?id_noticia=60655&anio=2007&mes=2&dia=13.

———. 2007b. "Los quichuas y Agip dialogan." February 2. http://webcache.googleusercontent.com/search?q=cache:z5ZuFcm505cJ:www.elcomercio.cpm/Generales/Solo Texto.aspx%3Fgn3articleID%3D79576+comision+asuntos+amazonicos+del+congreso+%2B2007&cd=1&hl=en&ct=clnk&gl=us&client=safari.

———. 2006. "La protesta se salió de control en Pastaza." March 16. http://www.elcomercio.com/solo_texto_search.asp?id_noticia=20154&anio=2006&mes=3&dia=16.

———. 2005a. "14 comunidades exigen que Agip cumpla un acuerdo." December 14. http://www.elcomercio.com/solo_texto_search.asp?id_noticia=9914&anio=2005&mes=12&dia=14.

———. 2005b. "Los kichwa y la compañía Agip buscan soluciones a un conflicto." December 12. http://www.elcomercio.com/solo_texto_search.asp?id_noticia=9625&anio=2005&mes=12&dia=12.

————. 2005c. "La petrolera Agip firma un convenio con 4 comunidades." May 2. http://www.elcomercio.com/solo_texto_search.asp?id_noticia=127036&anio=2005&mes=5&dia=2.

El Comercio.pe. 2011. "El congreso aprobó Ley de Consulta Previa a favor de pueblos indígenas." August 23. http://elcomercio.pe/politica/1150085/noticia-congreso-aprobo-ley-consulta-previa-favor-pueblos-indigenas.

————. 2010a. "Gobierno regional de Loreto: Reporte completo de Loreto." http://cadelectoral.elcomercio.pe/localidades/reporte-completo/160000/loreto. Accessed January 14, 2011.

————. 2010b. "Pobladores de la convención exigen dialogar con el primer ministro el martes en Quillabamba." August 7. http://elcomercio.pe/peru/619940/noticia-pobladores-convencion-piden-dialogo-primer-ministro-martes-quillabamba.

————. 2008. "Nativos matses rechazan actividad petrolera." December 14. http://elcomercio.pe/ediciononline/HTML/2008-12-14/nativos-matses-rechazan-actividad-petrolera.html. Accessed April 26, 2010.

Conservation International. 2006. "Mainstreaming Biodiversity Conservation into Oil and Gas Development." Prepared for *Biodiversity Opportunities in Latin America and the Caribbean: The Role of the IDB.* CI Policy Paper. July 28. Workshop at Inter-American Development Bank, Washington, D.C.

Crespo Plaza, Ricardo. 2007. "La legislación contradictoria sobre conservación y explotación petrolera." In Fontaine and Narváez 2007, 207–27.

DANE (Departamento Administrativo Nacional de Estadistica). 2005. "Censo general 2005: Nivel Nacional." May 22. http://www.dane.gov.co/index.php?option=com_content&view=article&id=307&Itemid=124.

De Ferranti, David, Guillermo Perry, Francisco Ferreira, and Michael Walton. 2004. *Inequality in Latin America: Breaking with History?* Washington, D.C.: World Bank.

De Janvry, Alain, and Elizabeth Sadoulet. 2002. *Land Reforms in Latin America: Ten Lessons toward a Contemporary Agenda.* University of California at Berkeley.

Delaney, Patrick. 2008. *Legislating for Equality in Colombia: Constitutional Jurisprudence, Tutelas and Social Reform.* Vol. 1 of *The Equal Rights Review.* London: Equal Rights Trust.

De la Torre, Carlos. 2006. "Ethnic Movements and Citizenship in Ecuador." *Latin American Research Review* 41, no. 2: 247–59.

Diario Hoy. 2010a. "La corte IDH admite a tramite el caso Sarayaku." May 6.

————. 2010b. "Sociedad Civil rechaza Ley de Participación." February 5.

Doughty, Caitlin. 2011. "Marching on Washington to Stop the Belo Monte Dam!" *Amazon Watch: Eye on the Amazon; The Official Blog of Amazon Watch.* June 20. http://amazonwatch.org/news/2011/0620-marching-on-washington-to-stop-the-belo-monte-dam. Accessed July 25, 2012.

Drimmier, Jonathan. 2010. "Human Rights and the Extractive Industries: Litigation and Compliance Trends." *Journal of World Energy Law and Business* 3, no. 2. 121–39.

Echandia Castilla, Camilo 1998. "Evolución reciente del conflicto armado en Colombia: La guerrilla." In *Las Violencias: Inclusión creciente*, edited by Jaime Arocha, Fernando Cubides, and Myriam Jimeno, 35–65. Bogotá: Facultad de Ciencias Humanas UN, Centro de Estudios Sociales.

Echandia Castilla, Camilo, and Eduardo Bechara Gómez. 2006. "Conduct of the Guerrilla during the Government of Uribe Velez: From the Logic of Territorial Control to the Logic of Strategic Control." *Analisis Político* 19, no. 57: 31–54.

ECLAC (Economic Commission on Latin America and the Caribbean). 2010a. "Foreign Direct Investment in Latin America and the Caribbean." Briefing Paper. Unit on Investment and Corporate Strategies of the ECLAC. Santiago de Chile: Division of Production, Productivity, and Management, ECLAC.

———. 2010b. *La inversión extranjera directa en América Latina y el Caribe*. Santiago de Chile: Naciones Unidas, ECLAC.

———. 2010c. *Social Panorama of Latin America, 2010*. Santiago: Naciones Unidas, ECLAC.

———. 2010d. *Statistical Year Book for Latin America and the Caribbean*. Santiago: Naciones Unidas, ECLAC.

Economist. 2011. "The Arab World: Awakening." February 17.

———. 2009. "Oil and Land Rights in Peru: Blood in the Jungle; Alan Garcia's High-Handed Government Faces a Violent Protest." June 11.

EIA (Energy Information Administration). 2012a. *Bolivia: Country Analysis Brief Overview*. August 23. http://www.eia.gov/countries/cab.cfm?fips=BL.

———. 2012b. *Country Analysis Brief Overview*. Independent Statistics and Analysis. http://www.eia.gov/countries/country-data.cfm?fips=PE&trk=m. Accessed March 9, 2013.

———. 2011a. *Argentina: Country Analysis Briefs*. Independent Statistics and Analysis. June 24. http://www.eia.gov/countries/cab.cfm?fips=AR.

———. 2011b. *Bolivia: Country Analysis Briefs*. Independent Statistics and Analysis . August 23. http://www.eia.gov/countries/cab.cfm?fips=BL.

———. 2010. *International Energy Outlook 2010*. July. Washington, D.C.: U.S. Department of Energy. http://www.eia.gov/forecasts/archive/ieo10/pdf/0484(2010).pdf.

El Espectador. 2010. "Casanare amenaza con impedir tránsito de tractomulas por ley de regalias." November 4. http://m.elespectador.com/noticias/politica/articulo-233150-casanare-amenaza-impedir-transito-de-tractomulas-ley-de-regalias.

Estadística Petrolera. 2011. *Producción fiscalizada de gas natural*. http://www.perupetro.com.pe/wps/wcm/connect/perupetro/site/informacionRelevante/Estadisticas/Cont_Estadistica_Petrolera. Accessed March 7, 2013.

ExxonMobil. 2003–11. *Corporate Citizen Report.* Irving, Tex.: ExxonMobil.

Fearon, James, and David Laitin. 2003. "Ethnicity, Insurgency, and Civil War." *American Political Science Review,* February: 75–91.

Finer, Matt, Clinton N. Jenkins, Stuart L. Pimm, Brian Keane, and Carl Ross. 2008. "Oil and Gas Projects in the Western Amazon: Threats to Wilderness, Biodiversity, and Indigenous Peoples." *PlosOne* 3, no. 8, doi:10.1371/journal.pone.0002932.g001.

Fontaine, Guillaume. 2009. "Actores y lógicas racionales en los conflictos socio-ambientale: El caso del bloque 10 en Ecuador (Pastaza)." *Facultad Latino Americana de Ciencias Sociales,* June 27. http://www.flacsoandes.org/web/busca.php?c=483&elTab=tbiblioteca&tipo=avanzado.

———. 2007a. "El Estado esquizofrénico: La política petrolera en áreas protegidas." In Fontaine 2007, 355–420.

———. 2007b. "La globalización de la región amazónica." In Fontaine 2007, 253–56.

———. 2007c. "Problemas de la cooperación institucional: El caso del comite de gestión de la reserva de la biosfera Yasuni." In Fontaine and Narváez 2007, 75–127.

———. 2004. "Análisis y evaluación de la gestión de los conflictos en el Bloque 10 (Ecuador)." *Observatorio Socioambiental,* January.

———. 2003. *El Precio del petróleo: Conflictos socio-ambientales y gobernabilidad en la Región Amazónica.* Quito: FLACSO; Instituto Francés de Estudios Andinos.

Fontaine, Guillaume, and Iván Narváez, eds. 2007. *Yasuní en el siglo XXI: El estado ecuatoriano y la conservación de la Amazonía.* Quito: FLACSO Sede Ecuador; Instituto Francés de Estudios Andinos; Yala; Wildlife Conservation Society–Ecuador; Centro Ecuatoriano de Derecho Ambiental.

Friedman, Milton. 1970. "The Social Responsibility of Business Is to Increase Profits." *New York Times Magazine,* September 13.

Fundación para el Debido Proceso Legal. 2010. *El derecho a la consulta de los pueblos indígenas en el Perú.* Washington, D.C.: Instituto de Defensa Legal, Seattle University School of Law.

Galeano, Eduardo. 1997. *Open Veins of Latin America: Five Centuries of the Pillage of a Continent.* Translated by Cedric Belfrage. New York: Monthly Review Press.

Galvez, Marcelo. 2007. "Indígenas del Pastaza acuerdan convenio con petrolera Agip Oil." *El Universo,* February 27.

Gamboa, Cesar. 2009. *Amazonía, hidrocarburos y pueblos indígenas: Un estado de la cuestión en el caso peruano.* Lima: Derecho, Ambiente, y Recursos Naturales.

———. 2008. *Camisea and the World Bank: A Lost Opportunity to Make Things Better.* April 1. http://www.brettonwoodsproject.org/art-561075. Accessed April 11, 2011.

García Hierro, Pedro, and Alexandre Surrallés. 2009. "La Declaración de Naciones Unidas y el territorio." In *Antropología de un derecho: Libre determinación territorial de los pueblos indígenas como derecho humano,* edited by Pedro García Hierro and Alexandre Surrallés, 18–32. Copenhagen: Grupo Internacional de Trabajo sobre Asuntos Indígenas and Alternativa Solidaria.

Gasparini, Leonardo, Guillermo Cruces, Leopoldo Tornarolli, and Mariana Marchioni. 2009. *A Turning Point? Recent Developments on Inequality in Latin America and the Caribbean.* Documento de Trabajo 81, Centro de Estudios Distributivos, Laborales y Sociales. La Plata, Argentina: Universidad Nacional de La Plata.

Gestión.pe. 2012. "En dos meses subastaran el mayor lote petrolero del país." July 25. http://gestion.pe/2012/07/25/economia/dos-meses-subastaran-mayor-lote-petrolero -pais-2008415.

———. 2011. "Las regalias de Camisea sumaron U.S.$92 millones en febrero." March 3. http://gestion.pe/noticia/722037/regalias-camisea-sumaron-us-92-millones-febrero.

Gil, Vladimir. 2009. *Aterrizaje Minero: Cultura, conflicto, negociaciones y lecciones para el desarrollo desde la minería en Ancash, Perú.* Lima: Instituto de Estudios Peruanos.

Gill, Nathan. 2011. "Petroecuador Boosted 2010 Oil Reserves by 50 Million." Bloomberg. January 13. http://www.bloomberg.com/news/2011-01-13/petroecuador-boosted-2010 -oil-reserves-by-50-million-update1-.html. Accessed July 9, 2011.

Gómez García, Rosario. 1995. *Diagnostico sobre la contaminación ambiental en la Amazonia Peruana.* Documento Técnico 15. Iquitos, Perú: Instituto de Investigaciones de la Amazonia Peruana.

González Guardia, Giancarlo. 2009. "The Camisea Project: Developing Legal Frameworks for Avoiding Social and Environmental Conflicts in Sensitive Areas." *Houston Journal of International Law* 31, no. 2: 213.

Gonzalo Tuanama Tuanama y más de 5000 ciudadanos. 2010. Constitutional Tribunal Sentence. Exp. no. 0022-2009-PI/TC. June 9. Lima, Peru.

Government Observations to the Consultation Law. 2010. Area de Tramite Documentario. Point 1. Presented to Congress on June 21, 19:20. Lima, Peru. http://clavero .derechosindigenas.org/wp-content/uploads/2010/06/peru-observacionesley-consulta .pdf. Accessed on March 12, 2011.

Gray, Andrew. 2003. *Indigenous Rights and Development: Self-Determination in an Amazonian Community.* Oxfordshire: Marston, Lindsay Ross International.

Grey Postero, Nancy. 2007. *Now We Are Citizens: Indigenous Politics in Postmulticultural Bolivia.* Palo Alto: Stanford University Press.

Gurr, Ted Robert. 2000a. "Democratic Governance and Strategies of Accommodation in Plural Societies." In Gurr 2000, 151–77.

———. 2000b. "The Etiology of Ethnopolitical Conflict." In Gurr 2000, 65–95.

———, ed. 2000c. *Peoples versus States: Minorities at Risk in the New Century.* Washington, D.C.: United States Institute of Peace.

Human Rights Watch. 2002. "A Wrong Turn: The Record of the Colombian Attorney General's Office" 14, no. 2 (B) (November). http://www.hrw.org/legacy/reports/2002 /colombia/. Accessed April 8, 2011.

Huntington, Samuel P. 1992. *The Third Wave: Democratization in the Late Twentieth Century*. Norman: University of Oklahoma Press.

IACHR (Inter-American Commission on Human Rights). 2012. *Pueblo indígena Kichwa de Sarayaku v. Ecuador*. June 27. http://www.lahora.com.ec/frontEnd/images /objetos/cidhsarayaku.pdf. Accessed August 8, 2012.

———. 2010. *IACHR Concludes Its 140th Period of Sessions*. Press Release 109/10. November 5. Washington, D.C.: Organization of American States.

IADB Inter-American Development Bank. 2006. "Operational Policy on Indigenous Peoples." February 22. http://idbdocs.iadb.org/wsdocs/getdocument.aspx?docnum =691261. Accessed July 29, 2011.

IEA (International Energy Agency). 2012. *World Energy Outlook, 2012*. Paris: Cedex; OEDC/IEA.

———. 2011. *Are We Entering a Golden Age of Gas?* Paris: International Energy Agency, 19–22.

———. 2010. *World Energy Outlook, 2010*. Paris: Global Energy Trends; OEDC/IEA.

ILO. (International Labor Organization). 1989. Convention concerning Indigenous and Tribal Peoples in Independent Countries. C169, 76th I.L.C. sess. (June 27). Entered into force September 5, 1991.

———. 1957. Convention concerning the Protection and Integration of Indigenous and Other Tribal and Semi-Tribal Populations in Independent Countries. C107, 40th sess., 328 U.N.T.S. 247 (June 26, 1957). Entered into force June 2, 1959.

INDEPA (Instituto Nacional de Desarrollo de Pueblos Andinos, Amazonicos, y Afro-peruano). 2010. *Mapa Etnolinguistico del Peru, 2010* (propuesta). Presidencia del Consejo de Ministros. http://www.indepa.gob.pe/mapa2.html . Accessed February 25, 2013.

Indigenous Peoples Issues and Resources. 2010. "Indian Federation of Pastaza Quechua Denounce Divisiveness Promoted by Talisman Oil in Peru." April 1. http://www .Indigenouspeoplesissues.com/index.php?option=com_content&view=article&id =4581:indian-federation-of-pastaza-quechua-denounce-divisiveness-promoted-by -talisman-oil-in-peru&catid=53:south-america-indigenous-peoples&Itemid=75. Accessed May 19, 2011.

INEC (Instituto Nacional de Estadística y Censos). 2001. *VI censo de población y V de vivienda 2001*. Quito: Instituto Nacional de Estadística y Censos.

INEI (Instituto Nacional de Estadística e Informática). 2010. *Perú Sistema de consulta de resultados censales: Cuadros estadísticos*. Lima: INEI.

IWGIA (International World Group for Indigenous Affairs). 2010. *The Indigenous World 2010*. Copenhagen: IWGIA.

Karl, Terry Lynn. 1997. *The Paradox of Plenty: Oil Booms and Petro-States* (1997) Berkeley: University of California Press.

Kimberling, Judith. 1991. *Amazon Crude*. Washington, D.C.: Natural Resource Defense Council.

Kozak, Robert, and Matt Moffett. 2009, "Peru Struggles to Defuse Amazon Violence with 50 Dead." *Wall Street Journal*, June 8.

Kraul, Chris. 2011. "Colombia's Caño Limón Pipeline Bombed: Ecopetrol." *Platts Oilgram Price Report*, March 1.

———. 2008. "In Colombia, Paramilitary Gangs Control Much of Guajira State." *Los Angeles Times*, August.

Kymlicka, Will. 1995. *Multicultural Citizenship*. Oxford: Oxford University Press.

Lara, Rommel. 2007. "La política indigenista del estado y el territorio huao." In Fontaine and Narváez 2007, 175–206.

Larrea, Carlos, and Fernando Montenegro Torres. 2006. "Ecuador." In *Indigenous Peoples, Poverty and Human Development in Latin America. 1994–2004*, edited by Gillette Hall and Harry Anthony Patrinos, 67–106. New York: Palgrave MacMillan.

Leal Buitrago, Francisco. 1991. "El Estado colombiano: ¿Crisis de modernización o modernización incompleta?" In *Colombia hoy: Perspectivas hacia el siglo XXI*, edited by Jorge Orlando Mendo González, 397–446. Bogotá: Tercer Mundo.

Linz, Juan José, and Alfred Stepan. 1996. *Problems of Democratic Transition and Consolidation: Southern Europe, South America, and Post-Communist Europe*. Baltimore: Johns Hopkins University Press.

Lizarzaburu, Javier. 2010. "Cronología de un desastre anunciado." *BBC Mundo*. June 3. http://www.bbc.co.uk/mundo/america_latina/2010/06/100602_peru_amazonia_cronologia_baguazo_rg.shtml.

López, Víctor. 2004. "Para entender el conflicto entre Sarayacu, estado y empresas operadoras del bloque 23: Apertura petrolera, desarrollo constitucional de los derechos colectivos y crisis en el centro sur de la Amazonía ecuatoriana." In *Petróleo y desarrollo sostenible en Ecuador: las apuestas*. Vol. 2. of *Las apuestas*, edited by Guillaume Fontaine. 153–73. Quito: FLACSO Ecuador.

López-Calva, Luis Felipe, and Nora Lustig. 2010. "Explaining the Decline in Inequality in Latin America: Technological Change, Educational Upgrading, and Democracy." In *Declining Inequality in Latin America: A Decade of Progress?*, edited by Luis Felipe López-Calva and Nora Lustig. 1–24. Baltimore: Brookings Institution Press.

Lucero, José Antonio. 2008. "Indigenous Political Voice and the Struggle for Recognition in Ecuador and Bolivia." In *Institutional Pathways to Equity: Addressing Inequality Traps*, edited by Anis Dani, Arjan de Haan, and Michael Walton Anthony Bebbington. 139–69. Washington, D.C.: World Bank.

MacNamara, William, and Jude Webber. 2010. "Accident Puts the Focus on Safety." *Financial Times*, October 13.

Marc, Alexandre. 2010. *Delivering Services in Multicultural Societies*. Washington, D.C.: World Bank.

Martel, Jean Polo. 2010. "Rechazan ducto de TGP en Santuario de Megantoni." *La República*, May 27.

Martinez Cobo, José R. 1987. *Study on the Problem of Discrimination against Indigenous Populations.* UN Doc. E/CN.4/Sub.2/1986/7 and Add. 1–4. New York: United Nations.

Martinez Novo, Carmen. 2009. "The Indigenous Movement and the 'Citizen's Revolution' in Ecuador: Advances, Ambiguities, and Turns Back." In *Outlook for Indigenous Politics in the Andean Region.* Washington, D.C.: Center for Strategic International Studies.

Martz, John D. 1987. *Politics and Petroleum in Ecuador.* New Brunswick: Transaction.

Mayorga Alba, Eleodoro. 2006. "Oil and Gas Sector." In *An Opportunity for a Different Peru: Prosperous, Equitable, and Governable,* edited by Marcelo M. Giugale, Vicente Fretes-Cibils, and John L. Newman, 387–407. Washington, D.C.: World Bank.

McDougall, Gay, Mrs. 2010. Statement by the United Nations independent expert on minority issues. February 12. United Nations Office for the High Commissioner on Human Rights. http://ebookbrowse.com/statement-expert-on-minority-issues-gay-mcdougall-doc-d309651.

Miller, T. Christian. 2002. "A Colombian Village Caught in a Cross-Fire: The Bombing of Santo Domingo Shows How Messy U.S. Involvement in the Latin American Drug War Can Be." *LA Times Sunday,* March 17.

Ministry of Economy and Finances of Peru. 2013. "Portal de Transparencia Económica." *Información Económica.* Consulta de Transferencias a los Gobiernos Nacional, Regional, Local y EPS. http://www.mef.gob.pe/index.php?option=com_content&view=section&id=37&Itemid=100143&lang=es. Accessed March 5, 2013.

Ministry of Energy and Mines of Peru. 2009. *Perú rompe record histórico en firma de contratos petroleros: San Borja.* December 27. Lima: Ministry of Energyy and Mines.

———. 2008. *Statistical Hydrocarbons Yearbook, 2008.* Lima: Ministry of Energy and Mines.

———, ed. 1999. "Exploration Activities." In *Statistical Hydrocarbons Yearbook 1999,* 24–25. Lima: Ministry of Energy and Mines of Peru.

Ministry of Mines and Energy of Colombia. 1999–2011. *Estadísticas de producción: Sistema de información energética. Producción fiscalizada de petroleo por campo.* January–December. http://www.minminas.gov.co/minminas/hidrocarburos.jsp. Accessed January 8, 2013.

Ministry of Nonrenewable Resources. 2011a. *Cuidadania de la Amazonía satisfecha por la asignacino de 350 millones de exedentes y de utilidades petroleras.* June 22. http://www.ecuadorinmediato.com/index.php?module=Noticias&func=news_user_view&id=148296&umt=ciudadania_amazonia_satisfecha_por_asignacion_351_millones_excedentes_y_utilidades_petroleras.

———. 2011b. "Estatales petroleras inicián modernización." May 12. http://www.mrnmr.gob.ec/index.php?option=com_content&view=article&id=1062%3Aestatales-petroleras

-inician-modernizacion&catid=3%3Anewsflash&Itemid=133&long=en. Accessed May 12, 2011.

MiPutumayo.com. 2011. "Tres municipios de Purumayo bajo monitoreo por atentado a Oleoducto Trasandino." March 29. http://miputumayo.com.co/2010/08/19 /tres-municipios-de-putumayo-bajo-monitoreo-por-atentado-a-oleoducto-trasandino/. Accessed March 29, 2011.

New York Times. 1998. "Shell and Mobil Quit Peru Gas Project." July 16.

Nullvalue. 1994. "Primera alerta a los colonos de Cusiana." *ElTiempo.com*, March 5.

O'Donnell, Guillermo A. 1998. "Horizontal Accountability in New Democracies." *Journal of Democracy* 9, no. 3: 112–26.

Office of the Ombudsman of Peru. 2012. *Violencia en los conflictos sociales.* Informe Defensorial 156. March. Lima: Defensoría del Pueblo.

———. 2011. Defensoría del Pueblo del Perú. Órgano Constitucional Autónomo del Estado Peruano. http://www.defensoria.gob.pe/. Accessed November 20, 2011.

———. 2009a. "Décimotercer informe anual presentado al Congreso de la República." January–December. http://www.defensoria.gob.pe/modules/Downloads/informes /anuales/informe-anual-13.pdf.

———. 2009b. *Hacia una descentralización al servicio de las personas: Recomendaciones en torno al proceso de transferencia de competencias a los gobiernos regionales.* Serie Informes Defensorial 141. Lima: Defensoría del Pueblo.

———. 2008a. *Resolución Defensorial Humanitaria No. 007: December 05, 2001; Organic Law for the Recovery of the Use of Oil Resources That Belong to the State, and Administrative Rationalization of the Debt Processes.* Official Registry 308. Oficio SAC-2008-115. Lima: Defensoría del Pueblo.

———. 2008b. *Uso o abuso de la autonomía municipal: El desafío del desarrollo local.* Serie Informe Defensorial 133. Lima: Defensoría del Pueblo.

———. 2006. *Pueblos indígenas en situación de aislamiento y contacto inicial.* Serie Informe Defensorial 101. Lima: Defensoría del Pueblo.

———. 2002. *Elecciones 2000: Supervision de la Defensoria del Pueblo.* Lima: Defensoria del Pueblo.

Orta-Martinez, Orti, and Matt Finer. 2010. "A Second Hydrocarbons Boom Threatens the Peruvian Amazon: Trends, Projections and Policy Implications." *Environmental Research Letters,* February 16.

Orta-Martinez, Orti, Dora A. Napolitano, Gregor J. MacLennan, Cristina O'Callaghan, Sylvia Ciborowski, and Xavier Fabregas. 2007. "Impacts of Petroleum Activities for the Achuar People of the Peruvian Amazon: Summary of Existing Evidence and Research Gaps." *Environmental Research Letters* 2. http://www.iop.org/EJ/abstract /1748-9326/2/4/045006. Accessed October 12, 2009.

Pacific Rubiales. 2009. "Where Talent and Knowledge Meet Opportunity." *Annual Re-*

port 2009. http://www.pacificrubiales.com/archivos/Reportes/anual%20reports/AnnualReport2009.pdf. Accessed March 16, 2011.

Partow, Zeinab. 2002. "Macroeconomic and Fiscal Frameworks." In *Colombia: The Economic Foundation of Peace*, edited by Olivier Lafourcade and Connie Luff Marcelo Giugale, 145–69. Washington, D.C.: World Bank.

Pearce, Scott. 2002. "Fueling War: The Impact of Canadian Oil Investment on the Conflict in Colombia." Working Paper Series. Centre for Research on Latin America and the Caribbean and York Universite, Ontario.

Pegram, Thomas. 2008. "Accountability in Hostile Times: The Case of the Peruvian Human Rights Ombudsman, 1996–2001." *Journal of Latin American Studies* 40 (February): 51–82.

Permanent Council of the Organization of American States. 2010. "Report of the Chair on the Twelfth Meeting of Negotiations in the Quest for Points of Consensus: Committee on Juridical and Political Affairs; Working Group to Prepare the Draft American Declaration on the Rights of Indigenous Peoples." Washington, D.C., February 22.

Perry, Guillermo. 2008. "High Inequality." *Americas Quarterly* 2, no. 2 (Spring): 50–59.

Perú21. 2002. "La convención paralizada por protestas." August 2. http://peru21.pe/noticia/617505/convencion-paralizada-protestas. Accessed January 14, 2011.

Perupetro. 2011. "Estadistica Petrolera, 2011." *Producción Fiscalizada de Gas Natural*. http://www.perupetro.com.pe/wps/wcm/connect/perupetro/site/informacion Relevante/Estadisticas/Cont_Estadistica_Petrolera. Accessed March 7, 2013.

———. 2010a. "Canon por hidrocarburos ascendió a \$51.523 millones en periodo enero–octubre." Press release. Lima, November 22.

———. 2010b. "Record en la contratación petrolera en el país." October 14. http://www.perupetro.com.pe/wps/wcm/connect/6950d9004450d2eaa441f5d5cbc162be/Nota+de+Prensa+14.10.10.pef?MOD=AJPERES&CACHEID=6950d9004450d2eaa 441f5d5cbc162be.

———. 2004–10. *Transferencia por canon y sobre-canon*. Lima: Perupetro. http://www.perupetro.com.pe/wps/wcm/connect/perupetro/site/informacionrelevante/estadisticas/canon+detalle?Canon%20Detallado. Accessed November 5, 2011.

Petroleum Economist. 2011. "Peru LNG: A First for South America." June 15. http://www.petroleum-economist.com/Article/2848461/Peru-LNG-a-first-for-South-America.html.

Philip, George. 1982. *Oil and Politics in Latin America: Nationalist Movements and State Companies*. Cambridge: Cambridge University Press.

Picq, Manuela. 2012. "Is the Inter-American Commission on Human Rights too Progressive?" June 9. *Aljazeera*. http://www.aljazeera.com/indepth/opinion/2012/06/2012658344220937.html.

Proetica. 2010. "Sexta Encuesta Nacional sobre percepciones de la corrupción en el Perú 2010." *Proetica: Capitulo peruano Transparency International; Ipsos; Ipsos*

Apoyo; Confiep. http://www.proetica.org/pe/Descargas/Proetica-VI-Encuesta-sobre -Corrupcion.pdf. Accessed November 23, 2010.

Proinversión (Agencia de Promoción de la Inversión Privada–Peru). 2011. http://www .proinversion.gob.pe. Accessed March 7, 2013.

Protección de los derechos fundamentales de las personas y los pueblos indígenas desplaza- dos por el conflicto armado o en riesgo de desplazamiento forzado. 2009. Auto 004. Constitutional Court, Bogotá. Sala segunda de revisión, January 26.

Quevedo H., Norbey. 2007. "Los veedores en la ruta de la muerte." *El Espectador*, Sep- tember 29.

RAISG (Red Amazónica de Información Socioambiental Georeferenciada). 2009. *Ama- zonía 2009: Áreas protegidas y territorios indígenas: Red Amazónica de información socioambiental georreferenciada.* http://raisg.socioambiental.org/node/106. Accessed July 7, 2011.

Reid, Michael. 2007. *Forgotten Continent: The Battle for Latin America's Soul.* New Haven: Yale University Press.

La República. 2009a. "Los heridos en hospitales de Bagua y Jaen ascienden a 169 [The Wounded in Hospitals in the Bagua and Jaen Regions Go Up to 169]." June 5.

———. 2009b. "Nativos Achuar acusan a petrolera Talisman de provacar crisis." Octo- ber 10.

———. 2006. "Nuevo derrame en gasoducto Camisea." March 6.

Reuters. 2012. "Talisman Energy Leaving Peru as It Continues to Shed Assets." Septem- ber 13.

———. 2010. "Chinese Firms Threaten Ecuador Arbitration-Letters." November. 12.

Romero, Simon. 2009. "9 Hostage Officers Killed at Peruvian Oil Facility." *New York Times*, June 6.

Ross, Catherine. 2008. "El caso del Proyecto Camisea: Logros y limitaciones de una coalición ciudadana naciente." In *Defendiendo derechos y promoviendo cambios: El es- tado, las empresas extractivas y las communidades locales en el Perú*, edited by Martin Scurrah, 199–268. Lima: Instituto de Estudios Peruanos, Oxfam América–Oficina Regional para América del Sur.

Royal Dutch Shell. 2003–10. *Sustainability Reports.* Amsterdam: Royal Dutch Shell.

Salazar-López, Leila. 2011. "Chaos on the Madeira. The Trouble with Dams in the Ama- zon." *Amazon Watch: Eye on the Amazon; The Official Blog of Amazon Watch.* March 25. http://amazonwatch.org/news/2011/0325-chaos-on-the-madeira-the-trouble-with -dams-in-the-amazon. Accessed July 25, 2012.

Salcedo, José Víctor. 2011. "En Camisea cocinan con lena." *La República*, January.

Santistevan, Jorge. 2000. *Elecciones 2000: Supervisión de la defensoría del pueblo.* Lima: Defensoría del Pueblo, Editorial e Imprenta.

Sawyer, Susanna. 2004. *Crude Chronicles: Indigenous Politics, Multinational Oil, and Neoliberalism in Ecuador.* Durham: Duke University Press.

Schumpeter, Joseph. 1962. *Capitalism, Socialism and Democracy*. 3rd ed. New York: Harper and Row.

SDPnoticias.com. 2009. "Experto afirma que Sendereo Luminoso es ahora un 'conglomerado empresarial.'" April 15. http://sdpnoticias.com/sdp/contenido/2009/04/15 /375822. Accessed May 30, 2011.

Semana.com. 2009. "Como el ejército se alió con el ELN en Arauca." May 26. http:// www.semana.com/nacion/como-ejercito-alio-eln-arauca/119765-3.aspx. Accessed May 27, 2011.

———. 2008. "Por qué se cayó la Ley Forestal?" February 8. http://www.semana.com /on-line/cayo-ley-forestal/109281-3.aspx.

———. 2002. "El nuevo narcotráfico." September 23. http://www.semana.com/nacion /nuevo-narcotrafico/65574-3.aspx. Accessed May 30, 2011.

Servindi. 2009a. "Perú: Amazónicos indician paro indefinido por incumplimiento del Congreso." April 8. http://www.servindi.org/actualidad/10257. Accessed March 8, 2011.

———. 2009b. "Perú: Lotes 135 y 137 se superponen a Reserva Nacional Matsés y a territorio comunal." December 29. http://www.servindi.org/actualidad/20856#more -20856. Accessed May 9, 2010.

———. 2008. "Perú: Señores del Estado y de Pluspetrol ¿Esto es o no es contaminación?" February 13. http://www.servindi.org/actualidad/3416/3416.

Shankleman, Jill. 2009. *Going Global: Chinese Oil and Mining Companies and the Governance of Resource Wealth*. Washington, D.C.: Woodrow Wilson International Center for Scholars.

Stewart, Frances. 2008. "Horizontal Inequalities and Conflict: An Introduction and Some Hypothesis." In *Horizontal Inequalities and Conflict: Understanding Group Violence in Multiethnic Societies*, edited by Frances Stewart, 3–25 New York: Palgrave MacMillan.

Sunday Times. 1995. "Under Fire: Shell Has Caused Outrage by Pressing on with a $2.6 Billion Pounds Project in Nigeria, Fuelling the Debate on Big-Business Ethics." November 19.

Thorp, Rosemary, and Geoffrey Bertram. 1978. *Peru 1890–1977: Growth and Policy in an Open Economy*. London: Macmillan/Columbia University Press.

El Tiempo. 2011a. "Dinamitan oleoducto trasandino en Putumayo." April. 2.

———. 2011b. "Ejército destruyó otra refinería ilegal sobre el Oleoducto Trasandino." April. 25.

El Tiempo.com.ec. 2010. "Corte condiciona actividad minera a consulta previa." March 23. http://www.eltiempo.com.ec/noticias-cuenca/37087-corte-condiciona-actividad -minera-a-consulta-previa. Accessed March 11, 2011.

Torres Dávila, Víctor Hugo. 2005. *Aprendiendo de los conflictos: Experiencias metodológi-*

cas de manejo de conflictos socioambientales en Ecuador; Plataforma de acuerdos socio ambientales." Quito: PLASA.

Total. 2011. *Society and Environmental Report, 2010.* Courbevoie, France: Total.

Total Foundation. 2010. *Activities Report.* Courbevoie, France: Total Foundation.

Transparency International. 2010a. *Annual Report, 2009.* Berlin. Transparency International.

———. 2010b. *Corruption Perceptions Index.* http://www.transparency.org/cpi2010/results. Accessed March 9, 2013.

Trivelli, Carolina. 2006. "Peru." In *Indigenous Peoples, Poverty and Human Development in Latin America, 1994–2004,* edited by Gillette Hall and Harry Anthony Patrinos, 199–220. New York: Palgrave Macmillan.

UNICEF-FUNPROEIB Andes. 2009. *Atlas sociolinguistico de pueblos indígenas en América Latina.* Vol. 1 of *Fondo Naciones Unidas para la infancia and fundación para la educación en contextos de multilinguismo y pluriculturalidad.* Cochabamba: UNICEF-FUNPROEIB Andes.

UNICEF–World Health Organization. 2012. *Progress on Drinking Water and Sanitation: 2012 Update.* New York. UNICEF–World Health Organization.

United Nations. 2010. *Promoción y protección de todos los derechos humanos, civiles, políticos, económicos, sociales y culturales, incluido el derecho al desarrollo: La situación de los pueblos indígenas en Colombia.* Special Rapporteur for United Nations on the Situation of Human Rights and the Fundamental Freedom of Indigenous Peoples. January 8. A/HRC/15/34. Human Rights Council. New York: United Nations General Assembly.

———. 2007. *United Nations Declaration on the Rights of Indigenous Peoples.* New York: United Nations.

United Nations General Assembly. 2008. "Informe anual del Alto Comisionado de las Naciones Unidas para los derechos humanos e informes de la Oficina del Alto Comisionado y del Secretario General." A/HRC/7/39. Consejo de Derechos Humanos: Séptimo periodo de sesiones. New York: United Nations General Assembly.

United Nations International Convention on the Elimination of all Forms of Racial Discrimination. 1999. "Concluding Observations of the Committee on the Elimination of Racial Discrimination: Peru; Concluding Observations/Comments." April 13. 54th session, CERD/C/304/Add.69.

Univision.com. 2010. "Parlamento de Ecuador rechaza consulta previa a indígenas sobre Ley de Aguas." May 13. http://www.univision.com/contentroot/wirefeeds/lat/8205834.shtml. Accessed March 22, 2011.

Urrea Giraldo, Fernando, and Carlos Viafara López. 2007. *Pobreza y grupos étnicos en Colombia: Análisis de sus factores determinantes y lineamientos de políticas para su re-*

ducción: *Misión para el diseño de una estrategia para la reducción de la pobreza y al desigualdad*. Bogotá: Departamento Nacional de Planeación.

U.S. Government Accountability Office. 2005. *Efforts to Secure Colombia's Caño Limón–Covenas Oil Pipeline Have Reduced Attacks, but Challenges Remain*. Report to Congressional Requesters, Security Assistance. GAO-05-971. Washington, D.C.: Government Accountability Office.

U.S. Senate. 1952. *The International Petroleum Cartel, Staff Report to the Federal Trade Commission, Subcommittee on Monopoly of Select Committee on Small Business*, U.S. Senate, 83d Cong., 2nd sess., Washington, D.C.

Van Cott, Lee. 2000. "A Political Analysis of Legal Pluralism in Bolivia and Colombia." *Journal of Latin American Studies* 32: 207–34.

Vargas Llosa, Mario. 2010. *The Dream of the Celt*. Translated by Edith Grossman. New York: Farrar, Straus, and Giroux.

———. 1989. *The Story Teller*. New York: Farrar, Straus, and Giroux.

Vásquez, Patricia I. 2011. "Energy Conflicts: A Growing Concern in Latin America." *Hemisphere: A Magazine of the Americas* 20 (Spring): 12–16.

———. 2005. "Chile-Peru Border Disputes Threaten Gas Talks." *Oil Daily*, November 7.

Velázquez, Fabio. 2003. "La descentralización en Colombia: En busca del bienestar y la convivencia democrática." In *Procesos de descentralización en la comunidad andina*, edited by Fernando Carrión, 127–77. Quito: FLACSO Ecuador, Organization of American States, Parlamento Andino.

Vélez Araujo, Fernando. 2008. "El paraíso del diablo." *El Universo*, May 23.

Vera Díaz, Julio César. 2010. "La política petrolera: Resultados y proyección años, 2010–2015." Powerpoint CAMPETROL presentation. February 10. Ministerio de Energía y Minas, Agencia Nacional de Hidrocarburos, Bogotá.

Vicepresidencia de la República de Colombia. 2002. *Panorama actual de Arauca y Casanare*. Serie Geográfica 13, Observatorio del Programa Presidencial de Derechos Humanos y Derecho Internacional Humanitario. Bogotá: Fondo de Inversión para la Paz.

La Voz de la Selva. 2010. "Obras planificadas para el 2010 no fueron ejecutadas por el Gobierno Regional de Loreto." December 12.

Water for the People. 2008. *Annual Report 2007*. Denver: Water for the People.

Wiessner, Siegfried. 1999. "Rights and Status of Indigenous Peoples: A Global Comparative and International Legal Analysis." *Harvard Human Rights Journal* 12 (Spring): 57–109.

Wikimedia Commons. 2013. Coat of Arms of the Eighteenth Army Brigade. https://commons.wikimedia.org/wiki/File:Brigada_18_coat_of_arms.svg. Accessed January 2, 2013.

Wirpsa, Leslie, and Thad Dunning. 2004. "Oil and the Political Economy of Conflict in Colombia and Beyond: A Linkages Approach." *Geopolitics* 9, no. 1: 81–108.

Wirpsa, Leslie, David Rothschild, and Catalina Garzon. 2009. "The Power of the Baston: Indigenous Resistance and Peacebuilding in Colombia." In *Colombia: Building Peace in Time of War*, edited by Virginia Bouvier. 225–45. Washington, D.C.: United States Institute of Peace.

World Bank. 2005. "OP 4.10 Indigenous Peoples." July. http://web.worldbank.org/WBSITE/EXTERNAL/PROJECTS/EXTPOLICIES/EXTOPMANUAL/0,,content MDK:20553653~menuPK:456185~pagePK:64709096~piPK:64709108~theSitePK :502184,00.html. Accessed July 29, 2011.

Yashar, Deborah. 1999. "Democracy, Indigenous Movements, and the Postliberal Challenge in Latin America." *World Politics* 52, no. 1: 76–104.

Yergin, Daniel. 1991. *The Prize: The Epic Quest for Oil, Money and Power*. New York: Free Press.

Zavala, Abel Andrés, Enrique Guadalupe Gómez, and Norma E. Carrillo Hidalgo. 2007. "El gas de Camisea: Geología, ecología y usos." *Revista del Instituto de Investigaciones de la Facultad de Ingeniería, Geológica, Minera, Metalúrgica y Geográfica FIGMMG* 10, no. 19: 113–19.

INDEX

Page references followed by *b* indicate a box, followed by *g* indicate a graph, followed by *m* indicate a map, and followed by *t* indicate a table.